UNC

THE

MYTH

OF

SPIRITUAL COVERING

Written by:
Steven Lambert, ThD, DMin

Published by:
Real Truth Publications

COPYRIGHT NOTICE

Unless otherwise indicated, Scripture quotations are from the *New American Standard Bible*, © 1960, 1962, 1963, 1968, 1971, 1972, 1973, 1975, 1977, 1988; The Lockman Foundation. All rights reserved. Used by permission.

Scripture quotations marked AB are from the *Amplified Bible*, Old Testament © 1965, 1987 by the Zondervan Corporation; *The Amplified New Testament* © 1958, 1987 by the Lockman Foundation. Used by permission.

Scripture quotations marked KJV are from the *King James Version* of the Bible. Public domain.

UNCOVERING THE MYTH OF SPIRITUAL COVERING

© Copyright 2016 Steven Lambert, ThD, DMin. All rights reserved under International Copyright Law. Contents and/or cover in whole or part may not be reproduced, stored in any electronic retrieval system, transmitted in any form by any means—mechanical, electronic, photocopying, recording, or otherwise—without prior written permission of the author.

Published by:
Real Truth Publications
P.O. Box 911
Jupiter, FL 33468-0911
Email: info@realtruthpublications.com
Website: http://www.realtruthpublications.com

ISBN 978-1-887915-25-0 (Ingram-LSI Print Version)
ISBN 978-1-887915-16-8 (Amazon-CS Print Version)
ISBN 978-1-887915-17-5 (NookPress Print Version)
ISBN 978-1-887915-26-7 (PDF Ebook Version)
ISBN 978-1-887915-27-4 (Epub Version)
ISBN 978-1-887915-28-1 (Kindle Version)

TABLE OF CONTENTS

CHAPTER ONE
INTRODUCTION AND BACKGROUND

This book is adapted from a chapter of my book, *Charismatic Captivation*—Authoritarian Abuse & Psychological Enslavement in Neo-Pentecostal Churches, first published in 1996. That book exposes the widespread problem of authoritarian abuse that has been flourishing virtually unabated for decades since it was first infused into the very fabric, foundation, and functions of the Charismatic/Neo-Pentecostal church during the false movement known as the Discipleship/Shepherding Movement (1970-77). The frequently quoted and alluded to volume spotlights the salient signs and symptoms of authoritarian abuse, dissects the fallacious doctrines behind it, and offers victims clear, concise steps for recovery from the psychological trauma and restoration from the spiritual damage they've experienced.

In the two decades since it was first released at the time of the publishing of this extract of it, *Charismatic Captivation* has been appraised and praised by Bible scholars and commentators, ministers, and laymen as the most comprehensive and convincing volume written to date on the particulars of the prevalent problem of Neo-Pentecostal authoritarian abuse, or what is also referred to as "spiritual abuse." Many readers and analysts over the twenty years since it was first published have come to concur with the somewhat audacious claim emblazoned on the back-cover blurb that despite being "disdained by defiantly unrepentant perpetrators of Pentecostal predomination, *Charismatic Captivation* is undeniably a genuine prophetic word ordained by God to which He is now demanding obedience."

If you have not read that book, I strongly recommend that you do for a better understanding of the context of the subject matter of this book and the larger issue of the widespread problem of authoritarian abuse transpiring particularly in the Charismatic/Neo-Pentecostal stream.

Owing extensively to the aforementioned Discipleship/ Shepherding Movement and the teachings that were promulgated during that false movement, hyper-authoritarian doctrines and practices have become cemented into the foundation, fabric, and functions of many churches, major segments of some denominations, as well as many of the protodenominational apostolic networks of churches, ministries, and ministers that have emerged over primarily that last four or five decades. The problem has become so widespread that it has now reached pandemic proportions in Pentecostal and Neo-Pentecostal streams.

One of the chief reasons these scripturally-condemned doctrines and practices have been able to proliferate and endure is that they have been going on for so long that the present generations of church-goers in these ecclesiastical groupings have been spiritually reared in church cultures where domination and control by church leaders is the norm and thus accepted as being normal and proper. The purpose of this book is to analyze against the foundation stone of Scripture, one of the foundational elements of this hyper-authoritarian ecclesiastical culture, demonstrate its irrefutable incongruity with Scripture, and disabuse believers from acceptance of and adherence to it, thereby liberating them from the invisible chains of psychological enslavement that have been holding them in bondage to the illegitimate authority structures of men that have captivated them.

By way of definition, hyper-authoritarianism is predominance or psychological control imposed by spiritual leaders upon their followers or congregants with respect to not only their involvements within the church or ministry, but also regarding the *personal* and *private* matters of their lives. Ministries and church-groups practicing this illegitimate domination employ various means and degrees of psychological indoctrination and coercion to compel congregants or adherents to subject and conform their personal activities, behavior, and affairs of life to the leadership-prescribed standards, rules, expectations, and collective corporate goals of the church or ministry. The purported pretext for the imposition of this scripturally-prohibited religious governance is an adulterated or perverted concept of ecclesiastical authority. Promulgators and practitioners adamantly claim that the mechanisms of manipulation they employ are a perfectly Scriptural system of "discipleship" or "spiritual training" in fulfillment of the role and responsibility of spiritual leaders to "make disciples."

However, the fact of the matter is this kind of "discipleship" exceeds by far the bounds and intents of legitimate, that is, Scriptural and Godly, authority. This kind of so-called "shepherding" is not that which is inspired by the Good Shepherd, but by His arch-rival, Satan, for it is nothing other than witchcraft and unauthorized meddling into the personal lives of God's Flock. It is blatant *misuse* and *abuse* of authority, and is Scripturally-prohibited usurpation of believers' God-given prerogative or right of personal autonomy. God, The Spirit, Himself declares in His Word:

> *For among them are* ***those who enter into households and captivate*** *weak women weighed down with sins, led on by various impulses, always learning and never able to come to the knowledge of the truth. Just as Jannes and Jambres opposed Moses, so these men also oppose the truth, men of depraved mind, rejected in regard to the faith.(2 Tim. 3:6-9).*

Indeed, the full context of this passage indicates what ilk of individual it is who engages in this kind of ungodly, self-aggrandizing governance over others, how others should treat them, as well as their ultimate fate:

> *But realize this, that in the last days difficult times will come. For men will be lovers of self, lovers of money, boastful, arrogant, revilers, disobedient to parents, ungrateful, unholy, unloving, irreconcilable, malicious gossips, without self-control, brutal, haters of good, treacherous, reckless, conceited, lovers of pleasure rather than lovers of God, holding to a form of godliness, although they have denied its power;* ***Avoid such men as these****. For among them are those who enter into households and captivate weak women weighed down with sins, led on by various impulses, always learning and never able to come to the knowledge of the truth. Just as Jannes and Jambres opposed Moses, so these men also oppose the truth, men of depraved mind, rejected in regard to the faith. But they will not make further progress; for their folly will be obvious to all, as also that of those two came to be. (2 Tim. 3:1-9)*

Such dominating ecclesiastical autocrats indoctrinate followers with fallacious, psychologically enslaving teachings, predicated on subtle twisting and outright perversion of Scripture, requiring them to strictly adhere to rules and demands set by the leadership if they are to have the approval of and be in the good graces of the leadership, as well as the collective group. Ultimately, submissive members are compelled, cajoled, and/or coerced to commit everything possible of themselves and their resources unto the support of the group's leaders, mission, calling, and purposes.

Nothing could be further from the clear intents and purposes of the genuine Gospel of Christ, which is not the bondage of servitude to men that hyper-authoritarian teachings promulgate and produce, but freedom:

> *So Jesus was saying to those Jews who had believed Him, "If you continue in **MY WORD**, then you are truly **disciples of Mine**; and you will know the **TRUTH**, and the **TRUTH** will make you **FREE**." (Jn. 8:31-32)*

> *It was for **FREEDOM** that **Christ set us FREE**; therefore keep standing firm and **do not be subject again to a YOKE OF SLAVERY**. (Gal. 5:1)*

Concerning the subject matter of this volume, allow me to speak plainly and directly: "spiritual covering" as theorized by those who teach, promulgate, and adhere to it is an absolute myth. No semblance of the version of "spiritual covering" taught by its proponents exists anywhere within the pages of Holy Writ (Scripture).

I will take it a step further and state straightforwardly and unambiguously: "Spiritual covering," in the vein that it is presented by its proponents and proliferators, is an unmitigated lie and complete myth! It is a complete fabrication concocted by the originators of these fallacious doctrines by which to facilitate and perpetuate their purely self-aggrandizing objectives of subjugation, domination and control of the sheep of God's Flock.

Indeed, what the Discipleship proponents refer to as "spiritual *covering*" is really "spiritual *control*." However, even the use of the word "spiritual" in this connection requires some qualification, because the only thing "spiritual" about this unauthorized control is that it is inspired by demon-*spirits* of deception and error. As we shall discuss later in Chapter Nine, what the Discipleship version of "spiritual covering" really is, is nothing less than **witchcraft** and **sorcery**. When the myth has been thoroughly debunked, as it will be within these pages, it will be clear that this doctrine of "spiritual covering," like all the other aspects of the Shepherding heresy, is a patently false "doctrine of demons" being manifested in these last days precisely in accordance with Holy Prophecy of Scripture that foretells of deception such as this being propagated by the inspiration of demons in the last days, leading to many falling away from the Lord into apostasy:

> *But the Spirit explicitly says that in later times some will fall away from the faith, paying attention to deceitful spirits and doctrines of demons, by means of the hypocrisy of LIARS seared in their own conscience as with a branding iron. (1 Tim. 4:1-2)*

With the foregoing as our introduction and backdrop for our discussion, let us now continue on our journey to dissect and analyze this matter of what I see as a diabolical, dastardly, and deceptive myth of spiritual covering or the "covering doctrine." It is the centerpiece of the heretical hyper-authoritarian teachings I've previously described, which are the bane of groups and churches that are ruled by autocratic leaders intent upon captivating a contingency of unsuspecting subservient believers to make their personal slaves to construct their private kingdoms and cash-cow businesses that they have they unmitigated gall to blasphemously call "churches."

Concerning the subject of Prophetic Function, the late Art Katz once eloquently wrote:

> A prophet not only identifies falsity, but he ruthlessly destroys it. There is something about his word that is like a fire. It is plucking up, rooting out and destroying before it is planting and rebuilding . . . .They not only just bring things into question, but they absolutely reduce it to rubble before your eyes. **For you to pick it up after that is to touch the unclean thing.** They have identified it and now you are stuck with that word.

Frankly, my hope for the message of this book is that after reading it the reader will have such a keen knowing of the utter falsity of the dastardly spiritual covering identified and addressed herein that to pick it up afterward would be to touch the unclean thing and by it be defiled.

Chapter Two
Five Coverings

W ith respect to our subject matter, the sum of what we will discover in these pages is that there are five "coverings" mentioned in the Word of God, four of which are authored or made by God Himself, and therefore are holy, good, and proper. The other covering is authored by Satan, and therefore is unholy, evil, and improper, and is instituted by Satan's human agents or cooperatives on earth in the natural realm.

The Covering of God's Presence

The first covering we'll look at is the covering of the mercy seat by the wings of the golden cherubim, which sat atop the ark in the sanctuary built by Moses at the command of and according to the pattern given him by God (Ex. 25:20; 37:9; 1Kgs. 8:7; 2Chr. 5:8). It was between the wings of the golden cherubim that covered the mercy seat that God appeared to Moses and gave him commandments concerning Israel:

> *"There I will meet with you; and from above the mercy seat, from between the two cherubim which are upon the ark of the testimony, I will speak to you about all that I will give you in commandment for the sons of Israel." (Ex. 25:22)*

When, as long as the tabernacle existed, the High Priests would enter the Holy of Holies once a year to sprinkle the blood of bulls and goats upon the mercy seat as a covering for the sins of the people of Israel, the Lord God (Jesus) would "appear" in a mysterious spiritual form by the Spirit between the two golden cherubim that were affixed to the ark of the testimony and suspended over the mercy seat. This mysterious manifestation of the Lord God served as a divine pronouncement that the shed blood had once again been received and accepted by God as temporary symbol of the satisfaction of sins of the people—a symbolic temporal propitiation of sin—until the coming of the Messiah who would effect the final shalom (peace) between God and mankind.

The Covering of God's Righteousness

The second covering we'll discuss is actually the first covering mentioned in the Bible, in the first book of the Bible, Genesis, the book of the beginnings, and then its spiritual counterpart is mentioned numerous times in the last book of the Bible, the book of Revelation. This covering is the most important covering of all, in that this covering—the covering of God's righteousness—is that covering that makes it possible for God to see and regard us as "holy and blameless before Him" (Eph. 1:4; see also, Eph. 5:27, Col. 1:21-11).

Man was originally created by God in *His* image and therefore was originally holy and blameless like God Himself. Thus, before the fall, Adam and Eve, because they were holy and blameless, had no consciousness of sin and evil, and therefore no shame, though they were naked, or unclothed:

*And the man and his wife were both **naked** and were **not ashamed**. (Gen. 2:25)*

But, then, tragically, subsequent and consequential to the fall:

*Then the eyes of both of them were opened, and **they knew that they were naked**; and they sewed fig leaves together and made themselves **loin coverings**. They heard the sound of the LORD God walking in the garden in the cool of the day, and the man and his wife hid themselves from the presence of the LORD God among the trees of the garden. Then the LORD God called to the man, and said to him, "Where are you?" He said, "I heard the sound of You in the garden, and **I was afraid because I was naked**; so I hid myself." (Gen. 3:7-10)*

The tragic result of the fall of man was that their soulish eyes were opened so that they now had a soul-consciousness of "good and evil," and through that soulish perception they now had an awareness or knowledge that they were naked, which produced a soulish shame. So, in an attempt to "cover" over that inward sense of shame, they sewed fig leaves together and made themselves loin coverings, not understanding that their shame was inward and could not be overcome by outward clothing covering their private parts. That was made manifest when they next "heard the sound of the LORD God walking in the garden in the cool of the day, and the man and his wife hid themselves from the presence of the LORD God among the trees of the garden." So also was the fact that man now was stricken with a soulish instinct to run and hide himself from God because as a result of his uncovered, unredeemed sin, he was now afraid of God: "I heard the sound of You in the garden, and **I was afraid because I was naked; so I hid myself.**" Unredeemed mankind has existed in that very circumstance ever since—afraid of God because of his spiritual nakedness before a holy God, which causes him to run and hide himself from God.

But God created mankind for the purpose of having fellowship with them. It is not His desire to be separated and alienated from humans. But, man yielded to the lies of Satan, the father of all lies, the tempter, and as a result fell into perdition, or spiritual apostasy. So, a "fix" to this tragic circumstance now was desperately needed, because God was not content to endure the separation that sin effected. So as a temporary "fix" until the "right time" (Rom. 5:6) would later come when God sent His only begotten Son to become the human Lamb God to die for the sins of the world, God slayed a lamb, shedding its blood for the covering over of Adam and Eve's sin, and made out of lamb skin an outward covering to cover over their soulish shamefulness as well.

> *The LORD God made garments of skin* for Adam and his wife, and *clothed them.* (Gen. 3:21)

When the Bible invokes the term "LORD God," it is referring to the second Member of the God-Head, God the Son, who, of course, would be manifest on earth in human form as Jesus, and become the Christ, the Messiah, the Lamb of God, whose shed blood takes away (remits) the sins of the world. Though the passage does not say it explicitly, because Jesus was, as John the Baptist, identified him, "the lamb of God," assuredly we can safely assume that the animal God slayed, shedding its blood to provide Adam and Eve the "garments of skin" for a covering for their nakedness and shamefulness, was a lamb.

Unless God had Himself "**made the garments of skin**" for the progenitors of the human race, Adam and Eve would have never known on their own, by their own knowledge, how to cover over their spiritual shame with which their conscience had now been permeated. They would have never understood that what their circumstance required was a "blood sacrifice" wherein a lamb must be slain and its blood shed, for "without the shedding of blood (there) is no remission" of sin (Heb. 9:22). And to be effectual, only the Lord Himself could slay the lamb, shed its blood for the covering over of Adam and Eve's sin and sin consciousness, for He Himself **was** "the Lamb that was slain from (before) the foundations of the world" (Rev. 13:8). What is so critical to understand and what I am trying to point out is that this act of providing spiritually fallen Adam and Eve with an effectual covering that was able to cover over their sin and sin consciousness was executed by Christ Himself at the beginning of human history in the Garden of Eden in order that they be restored to fellowship and relationship with God, otherwise the entire human race would have been damned and doomed with the very first humans.

From the beginning, man needed a covering for sin that could only be provided by God Himself. So, as it turns out, this one rather inauspicious verse of Scripture, Genesis 3:21, though it appears in the book of the beginnings subtly with no fanfare or pomp, is arguably the most critical verse in the entire Bible. Had it not been for what is described in this verse, there would be nothing of what transpired subsequently over the ensuing six-thousand years.

Nevertheless, Scripture makes it clear that the need for a covering for sin that only God Himself could provide was by no means a surprise to the omniscient Creator that somehow caught Him off guard, but rather He knew the whole matter of Man's debut on Earth could go no other way, and thus He made the provision for a redemptive covering for Man's inevitable sin and consequential fall before it transpired and even before He formed the foundations of world and the creation and placement of Mankind upon the Earth:

> *just as He chose us in Him **before the foundation of the world***, *that we would be holy and blameless before Him. In love (Eph. 1:4)*

Despite the mind-blowing loftiness of the concept, God's desire to have fellowship and relationship with His Mankind Creation was so strong that His provision to deal with the sin and sinfulness with which the human race was permeated consequential to the Garden fall and failure far surpassed the mere *covering* of it, which the provision of the shed blood of bulls and goats accomplished under the previous covenant, but rather under the new covenant, He accomplished through the shed innocent blood of Christ Jesus what the blood of bulls and goats could never accomplish–"For it is not possible that the blood of bulls and of goats should **take away** sins" (Heb. 10:4; KJV)—He completely REMITTED or REMOVED or TOOK AWAY the breach of sin and sinfulness, to the sublime extent of making redeemed mankind "holy and blameless before Him!" This unfathomable Divine doing, whereby he negated and countered the unspeakably horrific failure of the *First* Adam, He accomplished utterly and exclusively by the propitiatory shed blood and death of the *Second* Adam, the Son of God, Jesus Christ—"the Lamb of God who TAKES AWAY the sins of the world (Jn. 1:29)!

Witness and marvel at the New Testament passages that pronounce this utterly incomprehensible and mind-blowing transaction that the sin-damned mankind creation should be miraculously transformed into The Redeemed who stand before God holy, blameless, and beyond reproach:

> *just as He chose us in Him before the foundation of the world, that we would be **holy and blameless** before Him. In love (Eph. 1:4)*

> *Husbands, love your wives, just as Christ also loved the church and gave Himself up for her, so that He might sanctify her, having cleansed her by the washing of water with the word, that He might present to Himself the church in all her glory, having no spot or wrinkle or any such thing; but that she would be **holy and blameless**. (Eph. 5:25-27)*

> *And although you were formerly alienated and hostile in mind, engaged in evil deeds, yet He has now reconciled you in His fleshly body through death, in order to present you before Him **holy and blameless** and beyond reproach– (Col. 1:21-22)*

So, in view of all this, what happens to this original *covering* of lamb's hide that God Himself provided to cover the nakedness of the mankind progenitors, Adam and Eve, in the Garden of Eden, as delineated in the Book of the Beginnings, the first book of the Bible. Well, we see the lamb's skin covering God provided to cover Adam and Eve's shamefulness of nakedness, a covering for the natural man, in the last book of the Bible, the book of Revelation, is surpassed and supplanted by the white robes or white garments with which the redeemed saints of God, who have obtained by faith righteousness or rightstanding with God, are clothed and adorned:

> *'But you have a few people in Sardis who have not soiled their **garments**; and they will walk with Me in **white**, for they are worthy. 'He who overcomes will thus be clothed in **white garments**; and I will not erase his name from the book of life, and I will confess his name before My Father and before His angels.' (Rev. 3:4-5)*

> *I advise you to buy from Me gold refined by fire so that you may become rich, and **white garments so that you may clothe yourself, and that the shame of your nakedness will not be revealed;** and eye salve to anoint your eyes so that you may see. (Rev. 3:18)*

> *Around the throne were twenty-four thrones; and upon the thrones I saw twenty-four elders sitting, clothed in **white garments**, and golden crowns on their heads. (Rev. 4:4)*

> *After these things I looked, and behold, a great multitude which no one could count, from every nation and all tribes and peoples and tongues, standing before the throne and before the Lamb, **clothed in white robes**, and palm branches were in their hands; (Rev. 7:9)*

> *Then one of the elders answered, saying to me, "These who are **clothed in the white robes**, who are they, and where have they come from?" I said to him, "My lord, you know." And he said to me, "These are the ones who come out of the great tribulation, and they have **washed their robes and made them white** in the blood of the Lamb. (Rev. 7:13-14)*

> *And the armies which are in heaven, **clothed in fine linen, white and clean**, were following Him on white horses. (Rev. 19:14)*

> *Blessed are those who **wash their robes** so that they may have **the right to the tree of life**, and may enter by the gates into the city. (Rev. 22:14)*

Oh! How many words of extreme exultation, exaltation, and thankfulness pertaining to the glorious prize and precepts inherent in these passages telling about these fine linen, white and clean—whiter than any fullers' soap could make them, made so by the "crimson flow" of Christ's blood—*robes of righteousness* with which the Redeemed are forever clothed before God, could be here published, but such would require a book of its own! Suffice it to say that the wondrous works God wrought for the elimination of the breach Man's apostasy produced in the Garden in order to achieve eternal fellowship and relationship with His Mankind Creation is worthy of perpetual honor, praise, and worship of the Author and Finisher of this unfathomable plan of reconciliation, salvation, restoration, purification, and eventual glorification. Such a "sacrifice of praise" (Jer. 33:11; Heb. 13:15) shall the Righteous Redeemed spend eternity expressing to the God who has wrought such marvelous and inexpressible things!

This is the essence and denouement of the covering provided by God to His Mankind creation. It is the standard set by God for coverings. Those faux coverings human's purport to provide for fellows all pale into utter insignificance and ignominy when compared to the covering provided by God, for they can do nothing of what the Divine covering provides. Rather, they are nothing but complete counterfeits, completely void of anything beneficial or beneficent!

The Covering of Divine Protection

The third covering mentioned in the Bible is the temporal covering that the Lord Himself, not through any human proxies, provides unto every genuine believer during their life on earth. The full force of this covering, I believe the Bible indicates, is activated when a person surrenders his/her heart and life to the Lord Jesus Christ and is Born Again. This covering is a shield of protection and safety that a genuinely Born Again believer experiences during the course of his/her lifetime to shield them from the kinds of catastrophe and tragedy to which non-believers of the world are subject.

Psalm 91 is perhaps the most descriptive passage of Scripture regarding this divine covering. Verse four summarizes it: "He will cover you with His pinions (feathers of His wings), And under His wings you may seek refuge; His faithfulness is a shield and bulwark." The Psalms first verse informs us about the supernatural "shelter" that God's "shadow" provides unto those who abide in it:

"He who dwells in the shelter of the Most High Will abide in the shadow of the Almighty." The second verse is an exultation unto God extolling Him as a refuge and fortress for all those who put their trust in Him: "I will say to the LORD, "My refuge and my fortress, My God, in whom I trust!" The Psalmist further extols God in third verse for being the One "who delivers you from the snare of the trapper And from the deadly pestilence." The rest of the Psalm delineates the multiplicity of benefits of protection and safety the believer who truly puts his trust in God will receive as a result:

Psalms 91:5-16
(5) You will not be afraid of the terror by night, Or of the arrow that flies by day;
(6) Of the pestilence that stalks in darkness, Or of the destruction that lays waste at noon.
(7) A thousand may fall at your side And ten thousand at your right hand, But it shall not approach you.
(8) You will only look on with your eyes And see the recompense of the wicked.
(9) For you have made the LORD, my refuge, Even the Most High, your dwelling place.
(10) No evil will befall you, Nor will any plague come near your tent.
(11) For He will give His angels charge concerning you, To guard you in all your ways.
(12) They will bear you up in their hands, That you do not strike your foot against a stone.
(13) You will tread upon the lion and cobra, The young lion and the serpent you will trample down.
(14) "Because he has loved Me, therefore I will deliver him; I will set him securely on high, because he has known My name.
(15) "He will call upon Me, and I will answer him; I will be with him in trouble; I will rescue him and honor him.
(16) "With a long life I will satisfy him And let him see My salvation."

There are many more references in the Bible I could site regarding this divine covering provided by God to believers, but space and time simply will not allow it. Suffice it to say that this covering is one of the many benefits (Psa. 103:2) that inurs to every person who surrenders his/her life to the Lord throughout his/her lifetime on the earth. By no means does this mean that believers will not experience many troubles, trials, temptations, and tribulations during their lifetime—they will! Jesus said we all would: "These things I have spoken unto you, that in me ye might have peace. In the world ye shall have *tribulation*: but be of good cheer; I have overcome the world" (Jn. 16:33). The Apostle Paul taught the early Church believers and us today as well: "'Through *many tribulations* we must enter the kingdom of God'" (Ac. 14:22). Nevertheless, this covering of protection the Lord provides those who dwell in His shelter and abide in His shadow is a safeguard from the constant and unending devastations and decimation of catastrophe and tragedy many of the unbelieving and unsaved of the world experience during their lifetimes. Those of us who have put our trust in the Lord should always be mindful and grateful that no matter what tribulations and persecutions we have suffered, it literally could very well be worse, but thanks to God's providential protection is wasn't and isn't.

The Demonic Covering of Satanic Witchcraft

The fourth covering is the false Satanic covering of witchcraft that humans exert over other people who allow them to, in order to control and dominate them as pawns unto their own self-aggrandizing purposes and objectives. The latter is the covering that ecclesiastical autocrats, i.e., sorcerers, exert over their followers, both of whom are referred to in the following passage that describes this demonic covering as "rebellious children":

> *Woe to the rebellious children, saith the LORD, that take <u>counsel</u>, but not of me; and that COVER with A COVERING, but <u>not of my spirit</u>, that they may <u>add sin to sin</u>: That walk to go down into EGYPT [symbol of captivity in Scripture], and have not asked at my mouth; to strengthen themselves in the <u>strength of Pharaoh</u> [symbol of Satan and autocratic dictators in Scripture], and to trust in the <u>shadow of Egypt</u>! Therefore shall the strength of Pharaoh be your shame, and the trust in the shadow of Egypt your CONFUSION. For his princes were at Zoan [aka, Goshen, where Pharaoh met with Moses and Aaron; Easton's Bible Dictionary], and his ambassadors came to Hanes. They were all ashamed of a people that could not PROFIT them, nor be an help nor PROFIT, but a shame, and also a reproach. (Isaiah 30:1-5; KJV; emphases and parentheses added)*

We can see from this passage that Satan himself, not God, is the author of the false covering that it describes. It indicates that this covering is incapable of bringing any profit or benefit or help whatever to those who entrusted their lives to it. Rather, it brought the ostensibly unaware victims of this covering shame and reproach before man and God. We can deduce from this passage that such a "covering" is a complete abomination to God! The reason is because it is about trusting in man and the deceptions of Satan that are behind this "covering."

The following passage reveals why it is that Satan deals with "coverings" in his administration as the "ruler of this world" (Jn. 12:31; 16:11; NASB), "the god of this world" (1 Cor. 4:4) "the prince of this world" (Jn. 15:30; 12:31; 16:11; KJV) and "the prince of the power of their air" (Eph. 2:2), which is that prior to his rebellion and insurrection against God and consequential fall into utter apostasy and perdition, he was "the anointed cherub who covers"! Lucifer was the covering cherub! That's why he now deals with false and diabolical "coverings" by which he deceives those who will, despite the revelation and warnings given us in the Word of God, allow themselves to be duped and pulled into his clandestine schemes of deception!

Ezekiel 28:11-18
(11) Again the word of the LORD came to me saying,
(12) "Son of man, take up a lamentation over the king of Tyre and say to him, 'Thus says the Lord GOD, "You had the seal of perfection, Full of wisdom and perfect in beauty.
(13) "You were in Eden, the garden of God; Every precious stone was your covering: The ruby, the topaz and the diamond; The beryl, the onyx and the jasper; The lapis lazuli, the turquoise and the emerald; And the gold, the workmanship of your settings and sockets, Was in you. On the day that you were created They were prepared.
(14) "You were the anointed cherub who covers, And I placed you there. You were on the holy mountain of God; You walked in the midst of the stones of fire.
(15) "You were blameless in your ways From the day you were created Until unrighteousness was found in you.
(16) "By the abundance of your trade You were inter-

nally filled with violence, And you sinned; Therefore I
have cast you as profane From the mountain of God.
And I have destroyed you, O covering cherub, From the
midst of the stones of fire.
(17) "Your heart was lifted up because of your beauty;
You corrupted your wisdom by reason of your splendor.
I cast you to the ground; I put you before kings, That
they may see you.
(18) "By the multitude of your iniquities, In the
unrighteousness of your trade You profaned your sanctu-
aries. Therefore I have brought fire from the midst of
you; It has consumed you, And I have turned you to
ashes on the earth In the eyes of all who see you.

The Familial Covering

The fifth covering mentioned in the Bible is the only God-
ordained and proper covering relative to human relationships,
which is the spiritual covering that the husband and father provides over his wife and family. We will discuss that covering in
some depth in the context of the next chapter, in which I refer to
this covering using the alternate terms of Familial or Domestic
Authority.

CHAPTER THREE
BIBLICAL AND PROPER PRECEPT
OF SPIRITUAL COVERING

D iscipleship proponents point to a particular Pauline dissertation found in the Eleventh Chapter of First Corinthians as the primary purported proof-text for their concept of "spiritual covering." It will soon be evident, however, that, as is typical of the other aspects of Discipleship errors, the assertions made on the basis of these verses are the product of blatant perversion, distortion, misrepresentation, and misapplication of the true import and intent of the passage. The unfortunate effect of this corruption of Canon is essentially the same as that which inured unto the Galatians, which was that they became guilty of "deserting" Christ for a different "christ" and a different gospel:

> *I am amazed that you are so quickly deserting Him who called you by the grace of Christ; for a different gospel; which is really not another; only there are some who are disturbing you, and who want to **DISTORT the gospel of Christ**.* (Gal. 1:6)

Proofing the Proof-text

The following is the passage from which the concept of "spiritual covering," as well as several other assertions made by Discipleship proponents, is interpolated. It will be a basis for much of what we discuss in this chapter, thus I have set it in verse-format for easier reference. Also, I have added some explanations appearing in italics and parentheses to assist in understanding the true import of what is being said in these verses.

1 Corinthians 11:2-16:
(2) Now I praise you because you remember me in everything, and hold firmly to **the traditions**, just as I delivered them to you.
(3) But I want you to understand that Christ is the

Head of every man, and the man *(husband)* is the **head** of a *(singular)* woman *(wife)*, and God is the **Head** of Christ.
(4) Every **MAN** who has something on his Head *(Christ)* while praying or prophesying, disgraces his Head *(Christ).*
(5) But every woman who has her **head** uncovered *(not under the authority of her husband)* while praying or prophesying, disgraces her **head** (her husband); for she is one and the same with **her whose head is shaved** *(a symbol for a woman taken captive from vanquished enemies and forced against her will to become an Israelite's wife).*
(6) For if a woman does not **cover her head** *(allow the authority of her husband to cover and protect her from the spiritual deception of the fallen angels)*, let her also have her hair cut off; but if it is disgraceful for a woman to have her hair cut off or her head shaved, **let her cover her head.**
(7) For a **man** ought **NOT** to have his head covered, since he is the image and glory of God; but the woman *(wife)* is the glory of man *(husband).*
(8) For man does **not** originate from woman, but **woman from man;**
(9) for indeed man was not created for the woman's sake, but woman for the man's sake.
(10) Therefore the **woman ought to have authority on her head,** because of the *(fallen)* angels.
(11) However, in the Lord, neither is woman indepen-dent of man, nor is man independent of woman.
(12) For as the woman originates from the man, so also the man has his birth through the woman; and all things originate from God.
(13) Judge for yourselves: is it proper for a woman to pray to God with **head uncovered?**
(14) Does not even nature itself teach you that if a man has **long hair** *(type for "covering")*, it is a **dishonor** to him,
(15) but if a **woman has long hair,** it is a **glory** to her? For her **hair is given** to her for **A COVERING** *(a protection).*
(16) But if one is inclined to be **contentious,** we have **no other practice,** nor have the churches of God.

Now I don't want to be crass or unkind, but in my opinion a person must have a doctorate in absurdity or be totally brainwashed to read this text and in all sincerity and earnestness conclude that it says what Discipleship proponents and adherents assert that it says. Indeed, this text has been used as a premise for a number of pretty silly and bizarre notions, ranging from the role of women in the church all the way to the assertion that God is saying here that women are supposed to wear little doilies on their heads when they attend church. So let's examine this passage, and see what it really says and what it does *not* say.

Pertinent Peculiarities of the Language

First of all, an extremely vital fact to keep in mind in all Bible study and interpretation, and one which I must take a moment to point out here at the very outset of our scrutiny of this text, is that the Greek language, in which most of the New Testament was written originally, did not have a specific word for "husband" and "wife" as in the English language. Instead, the word for husband is the word for "man," and the word for "wife" is the word for "woman." The only way to determine whether the reference is to the *male gender* or to the *office of husband*, or likewise to the *female gender* or the *office of wife*, is by deciphering the intent of the context. This fact is absolutely critical to properly evaluating and understanding the import of the particular passage we are examining here.

So, with this in mind, careful scrutiny of the context of these verses on the backdrop of the whole of Scripture, leads to the unequivocal and incontrovertible conclusion that the words used here that are translated in many English versions as *"man"* and *"woman"* really should be *"husband"* and *"wife."* Validation of that is inherent in the fact that the principles evoked in this passage are limited in application to the husband and wife relationship. They are NOT applicable in the context of general interrelations between men and women, but rather only apply in the sphere of the husband and wife relationship.

Identifying the Subject and Scope

Once these peculiarities of the language are understood, the next matter of utmost importance is identifying the subject and scope of the passage we are examining. For reasons that shall become evident, it is vital to understand that the clear and unmistakable subject of this passage is the matter of *Domestic* Divine Order, that is to say, the order of authority existing among husbands and wives and their children, or to say it yet another way, the government operable within the structure of the FAMILY unit. *"Domestic Authority"* is the exclusive focus as well as the scope of this passage. The aspects and applications of the authority addressed in these verses are limited to the purview of that particular ilk of authority, and cannot be applied to any other type of authority.

Recognizing the true focus and scope of this text is crucial to comprehending its import. Not recognizing these parameters, or blatant disregard of them, whichever may be the case, has been a primary factor resulting in the formulation of the fallacious assertions adamantly proclaimed and staunchly defended by Discipleship doctrine proponents supposedly based on this passage. To be specific, the matter of "spiritual covering" is the heart of the issue. And, indeed, there is a type of spiritual covering that is addressed in these verses. However, what is critical is that, as stated already, the spiritual covering that is discussed in this context is **NOT** *Ecclesiastical* Authority, that is to say, Governmental Authority within the Church. Rather, *Domestic* Authority is the clear and unequivocal focus of Paul's dissertation here, which the Apostle makes evident in verse three by specifically identifying the topic of this portion of his letter and by expressing explicitly what it is he wants the readers to understand: *"But I want you to understand that CHRIST is **the Head** of every man, and the MAN(HUSBAND) is **the head** of a WOMAN* (his WIFE), *and GOD is **the Head** of Christ."*

Another way to characterize the focus of this passage, which the bolded portions of this verse bring out, is: "spiritual headship." However, the propensity of some to *"exceed that which is written"* has resulted in the misconstruing and misapplication of this perfectly valid truth and the manufacturing of a kind of so-called "headship" based purely in human imagination without any Scriptural foundation whatsoever. In point of fact, the only valid ilk of "spiritual headship" or "spiritual covering" there is, and the only one which is supported by the Word of God, is that which is being addressed here, which is the "spiritual headship" and "spiritual covering" the **husband** provides for his own wife as the God-appointed representative of Christ within the family unit. In no way, however, does this passage contain any evidence or corroboration of the sort of "spiritual covering" Discipleship proponents allege is provided by a **shepherd** to his followers. To extrapolate from this passage a pretext for some sort of "headship" interposable by "spiritual leaders" over subordinate believers is an act of gross distortion, convolution, and misrepresentation of the Word of God, as well as an act of blatant and extreme irresponsibility.

CHRIST—the Only Spiritual Covering for Every Man

Now as I stated initially, Ecclesiastical Authority is decidedly *not* the focus of this passage. Indeed, the only mention of the matter of Ecclesiastical Authority occurs in oblique references in verses four and seven, which actually state the very opposite of what the Discipleship/Shepherding proponents purport the verses say and the very opposite of the assertions they cite the verses as a proof-text for:

4 Every MAN who has something on his Head (Christ) while praying or prophesying, disgraces his Head (Christ).

7 For a **man** *ought NOT to have his head covered, since he is the image and glory of God; but the woman (wife) is the glory of man (husband).*

In verse four, Paul specifically states that, juxtaposed to the married *woman*, who must have a covering of spiritual authority, i.e., a spiritual "head," which role is fulfilled by her husband, any *man* who covers his Head with a "spiritual covering"—a human, surrogate, intermediary "head"—is bringing reproach, dishonor, and disgrace to his Head, because, as Paul indicates repeatedly in this text, the man's Head is Christ Himself. Thus, to characterize the import of the text in another, forthright fashion: in this passage, the Spirit is expressly prohibiting human, surrogate, intermediary spiritual "headship" in the case of MEN, in that Christ Himself is the Head, or "spiritual covering" *"of every man"* who is truly Born Again and has truly submitted to the Lordship of Christ over his life.

Notice also the phrase *"while praying or prophesying."* Praying and prophesying are the *spiritual* activities and functions in which believers are to engage. This phrase gives qualification to this statement, making its import to be that it is in the realm of **spiritual** activities and endeavors *in particular* that a *man* is NOT to have another human-being as his "head," or as a "covering," for that role and function is to be fulfilled by the Lord Jesus alone. Christ alone is qualified and capable of fulfilling that crucial role and function.

This is vital to the matter of the Discipleship error, because this has been one of the areas of greatest excess and abuse, in that many so-called "spiritual leaders" (especially laymen) in these in-house "chains of command" became extremely caught up in their newly acquired (albeit, illegitimate) authority, for which they were not properly grounded or adequately developed or sufficiently mature spiritually to properly handle, but which they nonetheless began to wield and intrusively interpose into the lives of their "subordinates," including their most private, personal, and even intimate choices and decisions. The outlandish and totally false hypothesis was that each of the multi-levels of "spiritual leaders" over the peonic, subjugated, and supposedly inferior believer were his or her "spiritual heads" and "spiritual coverings," and whatever communication or correction God desired to relate to the believer, He would relay through one of these surrogate "heads," and so-called "confirmation" of the validity and veracity of the communication would manifest in the form of unanimous "agreement" among all these "heads." Theoretically, if just one of the "heads" in the chain of "heads" did not have "a witness" for the matter, that meant the communication was not from or of God.

This "no witness" poppycock became a primary mechanism of control, manipulation, domination, and other more nefarious activities, in an array of circumstances ranging from preventing members leaving the church or group to sexually-oriented abuse under the color of spiritual authority. The gravely damaging effect of this absurd and wholly false theosophy and system of religious enslavement is well captured in the impassioned complaint of a former member of the Discipleship Movement responding to Bob Mumford's attempted conciliation with disjoined former followers:

> *"Saying I'm sorry wasn't enough.... **We had been taught that the men who led us somehow heard from God better than we did.** Even after we left the movement there was that hidden fear that they might be right and we were somehow less of a Christian and had failed God by not being **totally obedient** to them."* (Mumford Repents of Discipleship Errors, *Charisma & Life*, February 1990, pp. 15,16)

Though we are certainly to avail ourselves of the ministry God disseminates through Fivefold ministers, and though we are to maintain a compliant and cooperative attitude toward them, and treat them with due honor and respect, no mere human is ever the "head" or "spiritual covering" of any other man, especially; or woman, for that matter, because "spiritual covering" exists and is effectual only in the relationship of the husband to **his own** WIFE—no other woman. In other words, even a Fivefold minister—apostle, prophet, evangelist, pastor, teacher—is the spiritual "head" of **only ONE** *woman* on this planet—**his own** WIFE (if he is married)! That, my friend, is it! FURTHERMORE, a Fivefold minister is the spiritual "head" of **absolutely** *NO* **MAN**! I cannot state it any more succinctly or directly than that.

Spiritual Mediators

The premise of absolute submission is predicated on the hypothesis that the spiritual leaders are in effect (though most Discipleship teaching adherents would emphatically deny the attribution) "spiritual mediators" between God and their followers, who assume the role of hearing from God on the behalf of their followers. According to the premise, the followers are spiritually deficient and inferior to the leaders, and thus basically incapable of seeking and hearing from God for themselves and cultivating ongoing communion and fellowship with God, so they need a "mediator," someone who supposedly has a more elite status with God, to be a priestly "go-between" between them and God. The hypothesis is that the leaders are much more spiritual than the people, and therefore more capable of receiving from God what is best for their followers. By the way, if that premise sounds familiar to you, you are right, because in essence it is virtually identical to the theories upon which the surrogate priesthood and papal system of Catholicism were based, which totally supplanted and negated the personal priesthood of believers in the Medieval Church.

This whole matter of "spiritual mediators" is so totally ludicrous and such a complete affront to the truth of the personal priesthood of believers that every knowledgeable believer should be thoroughly disgusted and totally outraged at such an idiotic, outlandish, and even blasphemous notion. The Bible explicitly says: *"There is one God, and ONE mediator also between God and men, the man Christ Jesus, who gave Himself as a ransom for all...."* (1 Tim. 2:5). There is never, ever to be any "spiritual mediators" between God and men, except the Christ—Jesus Himself. The Man with the nailprints in His hands is the only true spiritual mediator between God and Man. All the rest are pretentious impostors! Jesus is the only Man who ever lived a perfectly sinless life, which was the requisite enabling Him to become the Spotless Lamb of God, the propitiatory sacrifice, typified by the oblational sacrificial lambs, which the Jewish high priests offered up for the sins of the people century after century.

So also was Jesus the true Spiritual High Priest, who natural high priests who offered up the sacrificial lambs year after year represented. Those that came before Him were the types and the shadows, the mere "eikons" [Gr.] (reflections) of the real. Jesus was the real, the source of the reflection. He **was** the Image that the types and shadows reflected. He was the true Sacrificial Lamb who took away the sins of the world. And, He was the true Spiritual High Priest (Heb. 3:1), who offered up the true Sacrificial Lamb—His own sinless life—as a ransom for all, once and for all.

> *And the former priests, on the one hand, existed in greater numbers, because they were prevented by death from continuing; but He, on the other hand, because He abides forever, holds His priesthood permanently. Hence, also, He is able to save completely those who draw near to God through Him, since He always lives to make intercession for them. For it was fitting that we should have such a* **High Priest**, *holy, innocent, undefiled, separated from sinners and exalted above the heavens; who does not need daily, like those high priests, to offer up sacrifices, first for his own sins, and then for the sins of the people, because this He did* **ONCE FOR ALL when He offered HIMSELF.** *(Heb. 7:2328)*

> *...we have such a* **High Priest**, *who has taken His seat at the right hand of the throne of the Majesty in the heavens, a Minister in the sanctuary, and in the true tabernacle, which the Lord pitched, not man. (Heb. 8:1,2)*

> *But when* **CHRIST** *appeared as a* **High Priest** *of the good things to come, He entered through the greater and more perfect tabernacle, not made with hands, that is to say, not of this creation; and not through the blood of goats and calves, but through His own blood, He entered the holy place once for all, having obtained eternal redemption. (Heb. 9:11,12)*

The point is that the true High Priest has now entered into the true Holy of Holies into the actual presence of God as the ultimate and only effectual Mediator on our behalf (Heb. 9:23,24). He lives evermore in the presence of God as our Intercessor (Heb. 7:25), having appeased His righteous wrath, having taken upon Himself the punishment due us, and having cancelled out our debt of transgressions that separated and disfellowshipped us from God. Hence, since Christ Jesus has accomplished the ultimate on our behalf before God, and perpetually lives in the presence of God as our spiritual High Priest and Intercessor, and since He has made peace for us between ourselves and God forevermore (Rom. 5:1), we hardly need human mediators between us and God.

His once-and-for-all sacrifice and entrance into the true Holy of Holies has granted us all equal access, free access, bold and confident access (Eph. 3:12), not only into the Holy Place, but also even behind the veil into the Holy of Holies, for each of us, even unto the very Throne of Grace itself, that is to say, the very Throne of *"the God of all Grace"* (1 Pet. 5:10). Of this access we are invited to avail ourselves freely, not coweringly but boldly, *"Let us therefore come **boldly** unto the throne of grace that we may obtain mercy, and find grace to help in time of need"* (Heb. 4:16, KJV).

To suggest that any human could do this for us as a mediator between us and God, is not only preposterous and absurd, but also an affront to Jesus Himself. It is blasphemy! Those who pose and interpose themselves as mediators between believers and God are fortunate that God has not struck them down dead! If Uzza, the loyal friend and servant of David was struck dead by God for merely touching the religious icon of God's presence, and if Ananias and Sapphira were struck down dead by God for having lied to the Holy Spirit, how much severer punishment would one deserve who is so blatantly blasphemous as to purport to be the spiritual mediator between God and men?

Those who are engaging in such Antichrist blasphemy against the Son of God would do well to repent, NOW, while God's grace and mercy are still extended to you! Do not mock this warning! I am convinced that in the coming days, many who continue to spurn and disregard God's warnings in this regard will suddenly fall dead in judgment from God, leaving behind a legacy of unfulfilled aspirations, consternation, mourning, and woe!

A Traditional Precept

It is evident from the initial verse of this dissertation we are examining (1 Cor. 11:2-6), that the Apostle Paul was not presenting any new concepts therein, but rather was only reaffirming *"the traditions"* (v. 2) that he had already delivered unto the Corinthian church as well as to all the other churches to which he had ministered.

Indeed, he commended the Corinthian believers for *"hold(ing) firmly to the traditions, just as* (HE) *delivered them to (them)."*

During the span of his ministry, Paul was the premier apostle, the primary spokesman on behalf of God, to the Gentile Church. In that capacity, he reaffirmed and reestablished in the New Testament churches those elements of the Jewish traditional teachings that were appropriate and applicable in the New Testament Age. Some of the practices that had come to be part of the Jewish religious traditions were purely the concoctions of men, and never the explicit or even implicit intents of the Lord. (Someone once observed that though God gave only *ten* commandments through Moses, by the time Jesus came, the various sects of priests required observance of some *ten-thousand* ceremonial and ritualistic *"commandments of men"* [Mk. 7:68].)

However, in the case of the spiritual government, protection, and leadership that the husband was responsible to provide for his wife and family, and the role of government and leadership men were to fulfill in Jewish society, this was one portion of Jewish tradition that indeed was congruous with Divine intent, and had not been denigrated or abrogated over the centuries. Moreover, in this portion of his lengthy letter of instruction and reproof to the Corinthians, the Apostle Paul reaffirmed and reminded them that he had delivered this precept as one that was valid under the New Covenant and was to be practiced in the New Testament Church, which he explicitly expresses in the sixteenth verse: *"...we have no other practice, nor have the churches of God."*

Jewish tradition always rightly held that the husband was the human spiritual *head,* or *government,* or *covering,* over his wife. This time-honored traditional precept was predicated on the order of Domestic Authority God had established within the first family unit of the Holy Race (Adam and Eve) subsequent to and as the consequence of their fall into apostasy, which was the direct result of the spiritual beguilement of the woman by the arch-fallen-angel, Satan.

The Weakness of the Woman

You see, despite the superabundance of boisterous protestations and brazen professions to the contrary being flaunted far and wide by the feminists and homosexuals bent on establishing a gynocentric society and deifying the female gender, and despite the pseudo-Christian, Jezebel-spirited feminists within the Church lobbying for gender-egalitarianism as a precursor to obtaining more and more authority and dominion, God did NOT create the genders with natural equality (albeit, He did create them with parity in terms of their status and standing with Him). Rather, the fact of the matter is that God created the female gender of human-being "WEAKER" than the male gender (1 Pet. 3:7). No amount of protestations or professions to the contrary will ever change that! So, rage on, dear hearts!

Not only was the female gender created *"weaker"* than the male *physically,* but also *psychologically* (a scientifically proven fact on both counts). Not only that, but, despite the fact that there is a higher rate of involvement among women in religion than men, in succumbing to the seductions and deception of Satan in the Garden of Eden, becoming *"quite deceived"* (1 Tim. 2:14), Eve openly demonstrated that the woman also was the "weaker" gender *spiritually.*

On this last statement, I can almost hear the uproarious and resounding retort of unrepentant, worldly-minded feminists masquerading as Christians: "But, the Bible says that in Christ Jesus there is neither male nor female!"

Of course the Bible says that! And, it means precisely what it says: that IN CHRIST JESUS—that is, in the glorified Spiritual state that awaits us beyond this present estate of natural humanness, wherein we have received our FULL redemption (Rom. 8:23), which is the redemption of our bodies (when the sin nature has been expurgated from our being), in that estate—there is no gender differentiations.

But, we have not yet attained unto that perfected spiritual estate. Though our human spirits are Born Again (Jn. 3:6), or regenerated, by virtue of being filled with the Holy Spirit, we still live out our lives in the natural realm, as *natural* beings. We have not yet been transformed into *spiritual* beings. Our souls and bodies have not yet been fully sanctified and permeated with the Holy Spirit. That will transpire when we are changed in the *"day of redemption"* (Eph. 4:30). Now, in this age, we have been given the Holy Spirit to reside *in* our spirits, charging our spirits with the *Life* of God, and *upon* us, granting us a minor measure of the *Power* of God as a "down payment," an "earnest pledge," which serves as a "security deposit," of what we *shall* receive when the Spirit fully pervades the part of our being that presently is not fully sanctified (2 Cor. 1:22, 5:5; Eph. 1:14; 1 Thes. 5:23,24). When that happens, we shall truly come into that estate in which we are *"in Christ"* (2 Cor. 5:17); and, we will have been literally *"transformed"* (1 Cor. 15:5053) into a *"new"* and different *"creature"* in which truly ALL *"the old things are passed away"* and *"new things have come"* (2 Cor. 5:17). Then, we shall have been *"transfigured"* into *"a different form"* as was Jesus on the Mount of Transfiguration (Mat. 17:1,2). Moreover, we shall have then entered permanently into that resurrected estate Jesus had entered when He appeared unto the two disciples on the Road to Emmaeus (Mk. 16:12), unto the one hundred and twenty in the upper room, and unto *"more than five hundred at one time"* (1 Cor. 15:6) after His resurrection.

This state of perfection in Christ—the state to which the Apostle Paul referred when he said: *"when **THE PERFECT** comes"* (1 Cor. 13:10)—has not yet come. That is why, as Paul explained, we only *"prophesy **in part**"* and *"know **in part**"* now, in this current dispensation (1 Cor. 13:9,12)—for we have not yet received the fullness of the Spirit and the accompanying *"powers of the age to come"* (Heb. 6:5) in their fullness and perfection.

Until this state of perfection—*"the perfect"*—does come, we are living in a condition called, "Born Again believer," or "Sonship." We have been adopted into the Family of God, we are Sons of God, God is our Father, but we have not yet received our *full* inheritance; only a portion of it. Collectively, we are God's "Betrothed," we are "engaged" to Him, but we have not yet been married to Him. That will take place at the Marriage Supper of the Lamb, which shall transpire at the end of this age when Jesus returns to claim His betrothed Church to be His Eternal Bride. This engagement period we are now in is a "waiting period" of sorts, a proving time, in which we are given the opportunity to prove that we are truly committed to eternal union with our Fiancée-Husband, if we are truly willing to become His wife, to become subservient to Him, to become His faithful and dedicated "helpmate," to be totally submissive and obedient to His authority—*"the authority of Christ"* (Rev. 12:10)—as our Head.

Until *"the perfect"* comes, and we are transformed out of this estate we are now in, in which we are *"IN the world, but not OF the world,"* in which we *are* saved (our Spirit *only* [Jn. 3:6]), are *being* saved (our soul [Jas. 1:21]), and *will be* saved (our body [Rom. 8:23]), this state in which we have been Born Again spiritually but still live in the natural realm, until then, we still abide in this human estate in which God created huMANs—*"male and female"* (Gen. 1:27). When we are transformed out of this human form, and the mortal puts on immortality, and the perishable puts on imperishability (1 Cor. 15:53), at the last trumpet of God—then shall we be fully *"in Christ Jesus,"* and then shall we have come to be as the angels, who neither marry nor are given in marriage (Lk. 20:3436), for they are genderless.

Until then, while we yet abide in the human state, as astute observers will recognize—there *are* men, there *are* women, the gender-classes *are* extant, and there *are* differences in those genders. The woman is still the "weaker" gender, physically (body), psychologically (soul; i.e., mind, will, emotions), and spiritually (spirit), whether in Christ (i.e., saved) or out of Christ (i.e., unsaved). This natural estate God has created is a fixed and immutable condition in this dispensation—*"until the perfect comes."* No matter how "saved" and "sanctified" and "spiritual" a woman becomes, no woman will ever "spiritualize" her way out of the female gender-class God created her in, nor override the Godcreated attributes of that gender, as so many "superspiritual" women seem to think they can or have. Until we are all *"changed"* (1 Cor. 15:52) at the last trumpet of God, even the most "spiritual" of believers will continue to abide in the humanstate and particular gender-class of our natural nativity in which God created us.

Until then, the woman, because God created her the "weaker" of the two genders, will continue to need the spiritual covering, protection, and leadership (government) of her husband, who is of the male gender, which gender, our text states, was created to be *"the Image"* (Greek, *"eikon"* = "reflection") and *"the glory"* (Greek, *"doxa"* = visible manifestation in the natural realm) of God; whereas the woman was *not* created to be the glory of God, but to be the glory of her **husband** (1 Cor.10:7, literal meaning).

The Purpose of the Covering

Subsequent to and as a result of the fall, which was the result of Eve being *"**quite** deceived"* spiritually and falling into transgression (1 Tim. 2:14), God placed an intense desire in the woman, to be covered and protected and led by her husband, saying: *"...your desire shall be for your husband, and he shall rule over you"* (Gen. 3:16). The word translated *"rule"* here means to govern. As a protection from spiritual attack, deception, and further transgression, God assigned the husband the role of providing government (covering) to his wife, to be her intermediate and human governor, or *"head,"* under Christ.

Verse ten explains that the woman's need for this protection is: *"because of the ANGELS."* Now although some expositors have confounded the import of this verse, it is really very simple. It is referring to the spiritual assailment perpetrated by the fallen angels (demons), especially in the form of spiritual deception, to which the "weaker" female gender has an inherent vulnerability and proclivity, as Eve vividly demonstrated with her verboten conversation she engaged in with the arch-fallen-angel, Satan, which resulted ultimately in the most dire consequence of her spiritual beguilement— the apostatizing of the Holy Race.

Though many people fail to assimilate it, the plain fact is that it was SPIRITUALLY that Eve was deceived. She was deceived by a SPIRIT—the devil, who seduced her into rebellion by means of a conversation in which she should not have engaged in the first place. Moreover, it was not with regard to some benign, unessential non-spiritual matter that Eve was deceived, but rather she was deceived with regard to the two most fundamental spiritual issues of all: 1) the choice between Eternal Life of God (Tree of Life) versus Eternal Death of Satan (Tree of the Knowledge of Good and Evil); and, 2) the veracity, integrity, and authority of God and His Word; i.e., is God God, and is His Word the ultimate, sovereign authority?

Thus, because it was *spiritually* that the woman was deceived, it is the *spiritual* realm in particular in which the woman needs protection. Hence, it is preeminently to protect the woman from *spiritual* attack and *spiritual* deception that God established the husband as the *"spiritual* covering" or *"spiritual* governor" over the woman, under the ultimate Headship of Christ. And, God has placed within the psyche (soul) of the woman an inherent intense desire—what the Amplified Bible goes so far as to call a *"craving"*—for this government and leadership and protection by her husband.

Paraphrased, the true thrust of what God was saying to Eve as the progenitor of the female gender of the Holy Race and to every woman who would descend from her in perpetuity in this regard in Genesis 3:16 was: "Eve, because of the vulnerability to the spiritual attack of the fallen angels that you demonstrated (in this exchange you just had with Satan) is inherent to your gender, in order to protect you and your genus-posterity from further deception and attack from the fallen angels—from this day forward....I have placed within your psychological makeup an intense yearning for your God-appointed husband and for his government, leadership, and protection over you, and a consuming desire to wholly dedicate yourself and your life to serving him as his select and suitable helpmate."

I believe God did indeed somehow imprint this consuming desire upon the tablet of the woman's psyche, or psychological constitution, and every woman realizes her greatest peace, joy, contentment, and satisfaction when this dedication to her husband is her pursuit. Conversely, it is when women rebel against this God-ordained innate foundational *"desire"* that they become discontented, malcontented, and miserable, and enter into various types and degrees of divertive and dissatisfying pursuits and deviant and demeaning behavior. But, when a woman becomes truly saved, and wholly surrendered to the lordship of Christ, as well as to the intermediate lordship of her husband under Christ, it is therein that she discovers and realizes optimum ecstasy and satiation.

What so many women, today especially, need to be reminded of is the foundational Truth delineated in verses eight and nine of our text: *"man does not originate from woman, but woman from man; for indeed man was not created for the woman's sake, but woman for the man's sake."* God created the man FIRST, and fashioned the woman out of the riven side of the man to make her a *"helpmate suitable"* (Gen. 2:20) unto the man. This gynocentric (woman-centered) society that these ungodly, perverse, lesbian-spirited, demon-possessed, authority-craving feminists are hell-bent on forcing upon the world, is the ultimate inversion and perversion of the entire order that God created for humanity. Like it or not, the world is NOT supposed to revolve around the woman, as it does today, the evidence of which is conspicuously manifest in the themes and images ubiquitously emblazoned across our television screens and pages of the deluge of print media inundating us at every turn, in which the female gender is exalted to the status of goddess and the female form is worshipped and glorified as divine. On the contrary, women were created by God to be *"helpmates suitable"* to their husbands— dedicated companions and collaborators, committed to colaboring with their mate toward the accomplishment of their God-given task and assignment: to subdue the earth and rule over it and everything on it (Gen. 1:26-28).

Women (and men) who truly and earnestly desire to be fully aligned—in thought, word, and deed—with God and His Word, Will, and Way, must, in this gynocentric age in which genderindependence is promoted and gender-enmity prevails, see to it that they give special attention and heed to what God said through this First Century apostle and prophet who scribed our text, which remains every bit as true, valid, and apropos today as it did then—that *"IN THE LORD, neither is woman independent of man, nor is man independent of woman."* God did not create the two genders of male and female of which the human race consists to be contentious rivals and mortal enemies of one another. In a time when racial hatred, or what I call *"ethnic-enmity,"* is pervading and threatening to consume humanity, we need also to recognize the *"gender-enmity"* that has been expanding as a consequence of the feminist movement, originally, and which now is being further fueled by the homosexual movement. It is conceivable that *gender*-enmity could ultimately produce an equally adverse end result as *ethnic*-enmity. My personal conviction is that Satan sees wholesale gender-enmity and homosexuality as his ultimate weapon in his age-long warfare against God that he continues to wage on the battlefield of human procreation. His intent in further expanding both of these demonic behaviors, along with continuance of the vile atrocity of abortion en masse is to inhibit and cause as much cessation of human procreation as possible.

Now before we go on, let me make one final comment concerning all that has been said here with regard to women, not to in any way mitigate, ameliorate, or appease, but simply to clarify. These are not the wrangling words of a woman-hater, nor the condescending chatter of a male chauvinist, but rather echoes of the sacrosanct colloquy of the Creator. All this was His idea, not mine. I'm merely God's reporter, recounting what He has said in His Word. If these concepts rub the cat the wrong way, as surely they will many, the cat needs to turn around! Which is another way of saying, repent—from all your worldly thinking, casting down vain imaginations, mere speculations and lofty human sophistry raised up against the knowledge of God, and subordinating every thought unto the obedience of Christ (2 Cor. 10:5)! When you do, the grinding, odious, discordant, and resonating, cacophony of these words will suddenly become euphonious, harmonious, melodious music to your ears.

CHAPTER FOUR
BASIS FOR AUTHORITARIAN ABUSE AND LICENTIOUSNESS

Again, I must emphasize that the subject of this passage clearly is NOT *Governmental* Authority in the Church. The dissertation is directed specifically to the matter of *Domestic* authority; that is, authority in the family unit. That is made evident in verse three, where the Apostle says: *"But I want you to understand that Christ is **the Head** of every man, and the man is **the head** of a woman, and God is **the Head** of Christ."* As I have already pointed out, another way to characterize the subject of this passage, which the highlighted portions bring out, is: *spiritual* "headship." However, the spiritual headship that is being discussed here, contrary to the assertions made by many, is not some sort of "universal" ascendancy, in practice and attitude, of men over women; nor does it speak to any ilk of Governmental Authority within the "ranks" of the Church. Rather, the exclusive focus of this passage is *"Domestic* Authority," which is the order of authority within the FAMILY structure, in human households. And in the household, within the structure of the family unit, there is only one head—the husband; not some "spiritual" leader; not *any* other person. The husband is the unequivocal head in *his* OWN house, and not in any other.

Moreover, the misinterpretation and misapplication of the import of this passage to the specter of general interrelations between men and women itself is the basis for one aspect of error inherent in the Discipleship doctrines that is of no small consequence. Specifically, the more radical Discipleship proponents have interpolated these verses to mean that *all* women, married or unmarried, are supposed to be "submitted" and subservient to *all* men, and especially to the "spiritual leaders" of their church or group. Furthermore, they contend Scripture prescribes that the purview of authority of the spiritual leaders of a church extends also into the home, and takes precedence over the authority of the husband in the family unit. It is this totally false assertion that is a common basis for much authoritarian abuse that is taking place right now in many more church-groups than what most people would ever imagine—most of it, at the time of this writing, yet to be exposed to the light of public knowledge.

For many years, I have known by the revelation of the Spirit that there are at least *scores* of cases in which these doctrines of demons are being used as a pretext and license for authoritarian abuse involving just about every kind of illicit and immoral sexual involvement by compulsion and seduction under the color of clerical authority possible. I predict that very soon God is going to see to it that the unwitting and confused victims of these heinous atrocities are liberated from their captivity, and that the perverted perpetrators of these despicable crimes and irresponsible violations of trust are publicly exposed, expelled from the ministry, prosecuted, and duly punished for their deliberate debauchery and violation against the lives and consciences of their exploited victims. Jesus said that it would be better for such perverted heretics who misuse the trust of their clerical office for such immoral exploitation that a millstone be tied around their neck and they be cast into the sea to drown, than undergo the Divine punishment that awaits them for having caused one of His little ones who had believed in Him to be so violated by such authoritarian abuse.

In the few months prior to the original writing of these words, a tempest of this kind was brewing in a mega-church in Metro-Atlanta, Georgia, involving a number of the top leaders of that church. When I first heard the accounts, I was not at all surprised, because some five years earlier, at a minister's conference I attended, the senior leader of this church was the keynote speaker. While he was speaking, I discerned a spirit of perversion upon him that was manifesting in numerous areas of his life and ministry. Immediately I recognized his teachings and beliefs were perverted. But, it was the authoritarian abuse involving sexual immorality I saw clearly by the Spirit that shocked me the most. And I simply knew within my spirit that, though at the time this man was highly regarded by some ministers and was experiencing extensive "success" in building a "network" of affiliated churches who considered him their "bishop," within a relatively short period of time he was going to be exposed and would "fall from grace." What I saw in the Spirit upon him was confirmed in a Christian magazine article (February, 1993) in which it was revealed that back in 1960, this man was defrocked and expelled from his denomination based on charges of immorality. The article was reporting about a public scandal that had recently erupted in which several female staffers had charged this man and his brother, an associate pastor, with authoritarian abuse involving sexual immorality. It is unfortunate that over the course of thirty-three years since the original exposure of his problem, this man apparently never received the deliverance he needed from the evil spirits of perversion vexing him.

I will add here a brief addendum regarding the scenario I described in the above paragraph, which originally appeared in *Charismatic Captivation.* At the time of the original writing, I did not feel, for various reasons, it was yet appropriate to identify the leader or the church I was talking about, however, since then the sad history of Earl Paulk has been widely reported and published. In the interim, even a number of his family members have made frank public comments about Paulk's sexual perversion; one nephew actually saying his uncle was a sexual deviant and pervert. Through court proceedings some years ago, it was confirmed through DNA testing that Donnie Paulk, who was reared by Earl Paulk's brother, Don, and his wife, was actually the biological son of Earl Paulk and Don's wife. If ever there was a man who became a symbol of the most egregious acts of misuse and abuse of ministerial authority as licentiousness and sexual perversion, it is Earl Paulk, who died an utterly disgraced man at the age of 81 on March 29, 2009, following a protracted and painful death from cancer.

The church Paulk founded and lead for so many years, that at its peak enjoyed thousands of devotees attending multiple weekly services, and "covered" hundreds of ministers and ministries around the world, eventually disintegrated to a handful of attendees of the mother church's services, was forced to sell the multimillion dollar campus consisting of the cathedral and annexed buildings to a Baptist church, and the global ministry once touted as the closest thing to the First Century church in existence is now essentially defunct, its legacy decimated, and its memory faded into oblivion.

The International Communion of Charismatic Churches (ICCC)

over which Paulk was appointed as the archbishop and brought into shame and disgrace by his vile actions is today virtually non-functioning under the leadership of a close Paulk associate who claims to have been the actual de facto administrator of the organization behind the scenes during Paulk's tenure. Paulk's successor as the ICCC archbishop committed suicide August 25, 2014 under a cloud of suspicious circumstances that have never been publically resolved.

Prior to his suicide, the organization and its leader were embroiled in a high-profile controversy sparked by one of its bishops who was the nephew of Earl Paulk, publically coming out of the closet as what he claimed was a life-long same-sex attraction and affinity, who resigned his church after his wife divorced him, and several months later, on December 31, 2014, married a long-time boyfriend, despite purporting that during his marriage to his wife he was not a practicing homosexual and had not had any ongoing gay relationships. The maelstrom that ensued entailed how the ICCC would respond to this bishop's actions and what its policy was and would be regarding LGBT related matters among its membership ranks and organization. The flames of the conflagration were fanned further when the then ICCC archbishop suddenly took his own life.

Since its inception, the ICCC was one of the leading promulgators in the Pentecostal/Charismatic stream of institution into those church segments their version of purported "apostolic authority," coupled with the dubious unorthodox theory of "apostolic succession" adhered to by numerous ecclesiastical sects extant today, which supposedly is an unbroken lineage of primal apostolic authority that began with the Apostle Peter—who under this theory is considered the first "pope" of the Church—and was transmitted uninterrupted via a succession of prelates through the ensuing twenty centuries of Church annals culminating with the current primary prelates of those ecclesial orders. Prior to the 20th Century the concept of "apostolic succession" was rejected by the vast majority of Protestant or non-Catholic ecclesiastical denominations and sects. The troublesome and troubling circumstances inherent in the ICCC history and its ostensible attempts in its beginnings at carnal legitimization of the Pentecostal and Charismatic streams by connecting it with the Roman Catholic Church, in my view, is a divine rebuke, demonstrating God's wrath with these unbiblical Nicolaitanism-like concepts and practices, whose deeds and doctrines Jesus Himself denounced in the strongest possible terms, proclaiming He HATED them (Rev. 2:6 and 15). For a detailed explanation of Nicolaitanism and how these hyper-authoritarian doctrines and practices relate to the subject matter of this book, I urge you to read Chapter Three of *Charismatic Captivation*.

Of course, there have been numerous other cases of well-known television evangelists and other high-profile inveterate ministers over the last few decades being exposed for having been involved in immorality and various abuses and misuses. It is all so very sad, and does indeed cast a long and ominous shadow of reproach upon the vocation of the ministry itself, in a day when more than ever before multitudes desperately need the real help that only Jesus can give and that is being offered through his true and faithful ministers. But, the most unfortunate thing is that there are still more of these kinds of revelations and scandals yet to come.

Moreover, in the process of time, it is going to become very apparent that the specter of authoritarian abuse and licentiousness perpetrated by wayward spiritual leaders is far more prevalent than what has ever been recognized before. Likewise, it will become just as manifest that the subject matter of this book—the heretical Discipleship doctrines, which are concerned primarily with false and fallacious concepts of spiritual authority—has been a primary underlying premise for much of the authoritarian abuse that has taken place among Charismatic and other Neo-Pentecostal churches and groups espousing these hyper-authoritarian doctrines especially.

The root-cause of the Discipleship heresy is the *"spirit of error"* (1 Jn. 4:6), which is a spirit of perversion, and the "spirit of error," unchecked, will eventually lead to a multiplicity of perversions in virtually every facet of the person's life in which this demon and its cohorts are manifest. In the process of time, this spirit will manifest perversion, corruption, and convolution in the host's spirituality and every aspect and attitude indigenous to their natural life—their morality, marriage, ministry, message, methods, motives, and monetary matters.

In respect to this type of authoritarian abuse, one thing that needs to be pointed out, however, is that it is not just individuals who have been victimized by this spiritually lethal perverse spirit, but so also has the collective Body of Christ, in that Satan has been sowing these weeds of heresy and tares of heretics in God's Field, thereby polluting and severely denigrating its produce, which was precisely his objective.

CHAPTER FIVE

THE FALLACY OF PERSONAL PASTORS

The adulterated concept of "spiritual covering" itself is problematic enough. Yet, its negative effect is increased by the fact that it is the predicate for several other, related elements of error comprising the heretical Discipleship/Shepherding doctrines and practices, one of which is the matter of "personal pastors." Indeed, this element has been the basis for at least as much excess, errancy, and authoritarian abuse as the others already discussed. To those who employ these practices for sordid purposes or with less than pure motives, the perverted concept of "spiritual covering" is sanction for a most insidious kind of unauthorized personal predomination and control of their subjects under the auspices of this very delusive and destructive version of "personal pastors."

As with most other elements of error with these and other false doctrines, this particular component is the result of perversion of a valid Truth. The essence of the erroneous concept of "personal pastoring" is that because the spiritual leader, along with the entire chain of leaders emanating from him, provides and in effect *is* the "spiritual covering" for his followers (which we have already shown to be a false hypothesis), the leader has not only the right, but also the duty to interlope into the private and personal affairs of the members of the group over which they reign. In essence, the leader becomes the equivalent of tribal chief to the group, whose final approval members of the tribe must have for most every important transaction and decision in their lives, with some variability depending on the particular group and leader. In many cases, members must receive authorization from the leadership for the most mundane transactions in their lives, including financial matters and purchasing decisions, matters of career and employment, housing, family, friends, social and educational matters, and just about every segment of the members' lives.

Now, of course there is a very valid role of Shepherding that Fivefold Shepherds (and all Fivefold ministers are under-shepherds, not just pastors) are indeed ordained by the Lord to fulfill on behalf of the Chief Shepherd (1Pet. 5:4), Jesus. The meaning of the word "shepherd" is to feed and care for, to lead and to guide, and that is the crux of what Fivefold shepherds are to provide on behalf of Christ unto the sheep of God's Fold.

As I have repeatedly indicated in various ways, what is involved in the case of the Discipleship/Shepherding teaching and practices, unfortunately, is a bastardization of the shepherding principle. And, the core of that corruption is that adherents of this teaching *"exceed what is written"* (1Cor. 4:6) by trying to impose their leadership authority and responsibility in the *natural* realm over individuals rather than limiting it to the *spiritual* realm over the administration of the ministry over which they preside.

It is absolutely vital for every minister to understand that the context and sphere of his shepherding is limited primarily to the spiritual. While Fivefold ministers may occasionally be able to proffer some inspired or experiential counsel and advice even regarding natural matters, their foremost calling and enablement is to feed, care for, lead, and guide the sheep of God's Flock spiritually and in relation to *spiritual* matters, not so much *natural* affairs. We are charged by God with the responsibility to feed His sheep *spiritual* food, to care for them with the *spiritual* wherewithal of the Holy Spirit, to lead them unto the one and only true Rock of their Salvation and Provider, Jesus, and after the pattern given us by the Chief Shepherd (Ps. 23) we are to guide them *"in the paths of righteousness,"* which is, the Way, Truth, and Life of Jesus.

When a minister routinely goes beyond the God-set, albeit, invisible, boundaries of his calling and purview of authority, which is the limitation of the *spiritual* realm primarily, and habitually interlopes into the *natural, physical* realm, interposing his own will in the ordinary private matters of his followers' lives, he is engaging in unsanctioned usurpation and illegitimate authority. In the process, he also leaves behind his legitimate duties, responsibilities, and sanctioning from God as an under-shepherd, as well as his effectuality. To take it a step further, a minister who engages in this sort of imposition and usurpation has essentially taken on the role, totally illegitimately, of the husband/father/head of those households and families over which he has imposed his authority; for, as the Scripture delineating true "spiritual covering" (1 Cor. 11:3-16) indicates, the role of headship (i.e., government or leadership) of a household or family in the natural, has been assigned by God exclusively to the husband/father of that house.

CHAPTER SIX
SPIRITUAL ADULTERY AND IDOLATRY

Another term for this illegitimate interloping and usurpation into another man's domain of authority is—*spiritual adultery*. Now to some this attribution will seem to be overkill and a bit melodramatic. Yet, in light of Scripture, it is neither. This is precisely what leaders who engage in these practices are engaging in—spiritual adultery. Allow me to explain.

God said the head of every woman is her husband, and every woman, at least every *Born Again* woman, has a husband, even those who are widowed, divorced, or never-married. Born Again women who for whatever reason do not have a human husband with whom they are living, are joined to and one with the Ultimate Husband, Jesus Himself (1 Cor. 6:17), the effectuality and efficacy of which fact is determined by the degree of each unmarried woman's acceptance of and faith in that fact. When a person other than the legitimate husband/head of a house invades the sanctity of that household by illegitimately interposing his own will and authority upon the woman of that house, that constitutes *spiritual adultery*. No person, man or woman, including ministers, is authorized to intrude into a household in this fashion.

It is with regard to this very sort of illegitimate authoritarian "home-invasion" that one particular New Testament passage alludes and admonishes with especial attribution to the "last days" in which we are now living:

> But realize this, that **in the last days** there will set in perilous times of great stress and trouble—hard to deal with and hard to bear. For people will be **lovers of self and [utterly] self-centered**, lovers of money and aroused by an inordinate (greedy) desire for wealth, proud and arrogant and contemptuous boasters. They will be **abusive** (blasphemous, scoffers), disobedient to parents, ungrateful, unholy and profane. [They will be] treacherous (betrayers), rash [and] **inflated with self-conceit**.

[They will be] lovers of sensual pleasures and vain amusements more than and rather than lovers of God. For [although] they hold a form of piety (true religion), they deny and reject and are strangers to the power of it—their conduct belies the genuineness of their profession. AVOID [ALL] SUCH PEOPLE— TURN AWAY FROM THEM. FOR AMONG THEM ARE THOSE WHO <u>WORM THEIR WAY INTO HOMES</u> AND CAPTIVATE SILLY AND WEAK-NATURED AND SPIRITUALLY DWARFED WOMEN, LOADED DOWN WITH [THE BURDEN OF THEIR] SINS, [AND EASILY] SWAYED AND LED AWAY BY VARIOUS EVIL DESIRES AND SEDUCTIVE IMPULSES. [These weak women will listen to anybody who will teach them]; they are forever inquiring and getting information, but are never able to arrive at a recognition and knowledge of the Truth. Now just as Jannes and Jambres were hostile to and resisted Moses, so THESE MEN ALSO ARE HOSTILE TO AND OPPOSE THE TRUTH. THEY HAVE DEPRAVED AND DISTORTED MINDS, AND ARE REPROBATE AND COUNTERFEIT AND TO BE REJECTED AS FAR AS THE FAITH IS CONCERNED....BUT THEY WILL NOT GET VERY FAR, FOR THEIR RASH FOLLY WILL BECOME OBVIOUS TO EVERYBODY, as was that of those [magicians mentioned]. (2 Tim. 3:1-9, A.B.)

I have alluded already to the fact that these false concepts of "spiritual covering" mixed with the "absolute submission" concept makes for an extremely poisonous and potentially lethal rue, which almost invariably eventuates into various forms of authoritarian abuse that frequently entails some kind of illicit sexual exploitation. This, of course, by Bible-definition, is physical fornication and *sexual* adultery, which obviously is utterly sinful and damning, not to mention the horrendous natural and spiritual consequences such abominable abuse and exploitation engender. Nevertheless, though it may be hard to imagine, the fact is that in these situations where leaders illegitimately interlope into the private affairs of their followers, usurping the role of the husband, even in those cases in which no physical fornication and *sexual* adultery have yet occurred, the "*spiritual* adultery" that has been committed is even more heinous and abominable and will produce even graver consequences, both spiritually and in the natural.

The reason spiritual adultery of this nature is such a grievous offense to God is that it is His authority, albeit, intermediated in the case of the married woman by a human husband, that is being usurped. The true spiritual Husband is Christ, and it is His betrothed that is being assailed when one of His sheep is abused and exploited. Thus, spiritual adultery carries with it an even greater judgment than sexual adultery for the unrepentant offender.

Spiritual Idolatry

Abhorrent as it is, that these Discipleship/Shepherding doctrines and practices constitute spiritual adultery, there is yet another offense they abet that in terms of gravity may even surpass spiritual adultery. In addition to spiritual adultery, adherents and practitioners of this false theosophy are also fostering and participating in "spiritual *idolatry*" as well.

These doctrines are idolatrous for two related reasons. One, because they lead people away from the objective of whole and complete trust in God alone as the ultimate Source of supply of all things. And, two, because in addition to leading people away from trust in God, they also lead people to put their faith, hope, and trust in mere flesh and bone human leaders for the things God insists we look to Him for, many of the particulars of which I have already addressed.

To merely call idolatry "sin," though it certainly is, somehow seems an extreme understatement, for it is the ultimate affront unto God. Yet, arguably, it is the most pervasive sin of all today among professing believers. Contributing to the prevalence of idolatry within Christendom, no doubt, is the common perception by many that idolatry is something that occurs only in underdeveloped, far-away, foreign lands, or that it is something relegated mostly to ancient civilizations of past ages, while nothing could be further from the truth.

In Galatians 5:20, the Apostle Paul by inspiration of the Holy Spirit listed "idolatry" as one of the fundamental elements of evil comprising the carnal nature, or sin nature, which actually is the nature of the devil himself, and which is also alluded to as the "spirit of disobedience"—the *"spirit that is now working in the sons of disobedience"* (Eph. 2:2). So, in other words, because the carnal nature is common to every human, idolatry, then, is a basic tendency of every person ever born.

In simplistic terms, idolatry is making something or someone that to which we look to bring happiness, peace, fulfillment, contentment, and all the things only God is supposed to provide us, which in essence is the definition of a false god.

To put it another way, idolatry is fashioning and forming false gods, or idols, out of one's own vain imaginations. Indeed, idols are really always imaginary, existing solely in the human mind and thoughts. Again by inspiration of the Spirit, in another place, Paul states categorically that those possessing true Spiritual knowledge and understanding *"know that there is no such thing as an idol* (false god), *and that there is no God but one"* (1 Cor. 8:4). False gods are false because they really do not exist, except in the mind of the idolater.

Idolatry in actuality then is merely the product of human thinking, manufactured in the factory of the human mind. It is the act of creating an abstract god within the deep, dark void of human reasoning. At bottom, all idolatry is "mind-idolatry," for it is primarily in the mind that all idolatry exists. Succinctly stated, the basis of idolatry is "stinkin' thinkin'."

Moreover, the ilk of idolatry that bona fide believers are most guilty of committing even routinely, though unwittingly, is the idolatry of holding to false and contrived ideas about God that in fact are wholly incongruous with what He Himself has revealed in His Word concerning His Divine Nature, Will, and Ways. When it is all distilled down, idolatry is the ultimate form of arrogance and self-righteousness, for it supplants God and His Word, Will, and Way, and puts in His place a false, humanly formed and fashioned god, one made in our own image and after our own likeness, to affirm and hallow our own humanly contrived ideas and concepts. Thus, idolatry, in my view, is the ultimate offense that the human heart can commit against a Holy and Sovereign God.

A.W. Tozer (1897-1963), who was the pastor of the Christian and Missionary Alliance Church in Toronto and Chicago for a number of years, was also editor of the CMA's official organ, *Alliance Weekly*, as well as a prolific author of books. His spiritual acumen was so highly regarded by his colleagues that many esteemed him a twentieth-century prophet. Despite all his prodigious achievements, he was perhaps best known for his personal intimacy with God, and his book, *The Knowledge of the Holy* (Harper

& Row), was a collection of some of his most outstanding messages related to knowing God in personal intimacy. So profound and insightful are his comments regarding the subject of idolatry, as well as exquisitely and eloquently articulated, that they could scarcely be improved upon, making direct quotation the only fitting means of reportage. The following are excerpts of his commentary, the order of which I have taken the liberty of rearranging to better serve our purposes here:

"Let us beware lest we in our pride accept the erroneous notion that idolatry consists only in kneeling before visible objects of adoration, and that civilized peoples are therefore free from it."

"The essence of idolatry is the entertainment of thoughts about God that are unworthy of Him. It begins in the mind and may be present where no overt act of worship has taken place. 'When they knew God,' wrote Paul, 'they glorified him not as God, neither were thankful; but became vain in their imaginations, and their foolish heart was darkened.'"

"Among the sins to which the human heart is prone, hardly any other is more hateful to God than idolatry, for idolatry is at bottom a libel on His character. The idolatrous heart assumes that God is other than He is—in itself a monstrous sin—and substitutes for the true God one made after its own likeness."

"A god begotten in the shadows of a fallen heart will quite naturally be no true likeness of the true God."

"Wrong ideas about God are not only the fountain from which the polluted waters of idolatry flow; they are themselves idolatrous. The idolater simply imagines things about God and acts as if they were true."

"Perverted notions about God soon rot the religion in which they appear. The long career of Israel demonstrates this clearly enough, and the history of the Church confirms it."

All false doctrine is, in essence, an assemblage of "wrong ideas about God" and "perverted notions about God," as Tozer put it. How profound and Scriptural is his statement: "**Wrong ideas** about God are not only the fountain from which the polluted waters of idolatry flow; they are themselves idolatrous," for "polluted waters" is a metaphor evoked in Scripture to represent false teaching. Indeed, false teaching is by no means, as some seem to believe, a harmless or inconsequential phenomenon, but rather polluted waters can be lethal, both in the natural and the spiritual.

False teaching, which in essence is substituting human ideas and sophistry for the absolute Truth of God's Mind, in fact IS idolatry. *Idolatry* and *false teaching* are synonymous terms. Idolatry always has associated with it some form of false teaching, and false teaching is always an ilk of idolatry. As Tozer so brilliantly articulated it: "The idolater simply imagines things about God and acts as if they were true." In other words, the person engaging in idolatry simply contrives his own doctrine concerning spiritual matters and the composition of "truth," and conducts his life based on those determinations even though they are not congruous with the real Truth that emanates from and is defined by God as Truth in His Word.

CHAPTER SEVEN
THE DANGER OF ZEAL WITHOUT KNOWLEDGE

A rather ironic and curious characteristic of the idolatry of false teaching is that essentially it is *"zeal without knowledge."* It is quite common for those caught in the throes of deception and false doctrine to be quite zealous and ardent in their spiritual pursuits. Where false teaching is being propagated—the perpetrators and the adherents commonly are fervently dedicated to their church-group and its purposes, beliefs, and goals. In fact, it is this zealousness by participants in aberrant and cultlike religious groups that makes it extremely difficult for caring bystanders to: one, fully recognize and realize the existence of error and errancy; two, to take serious the potential for spiritual and psychological injury and ruin; and, three, to recognize the need for and actually effect appropriate remedial action.

Certainly, this is the case with those who are being duped by these fallacious Discipleship/Shepherding doctrines. They are often very zealous and even marginally fanatical in their spiritual pursuits. And, in a day when there is far too little fervency for the things of God, most any of us are understandably reluctant to do anything that might douse the fire of someone who *is* on fire ostensibly for God.

The Apostle Paul, speaking of his fellow countrymen, the Jews, said, *"For I bear them witness that **they have a ZEAL FOR GOD...**"* (Rom. 10:2). He was saying that the Jews' zeal for God was genuine and sincere, and certainly no people had more religious zeal than the Jews until then. Nevertheless, their zeal, he went on to say, was *"not in accordance with **knowledge.**"* They had "zeal without knowledge." Their zeal, though extremely fervent, genuine, and unquestionably sincere, nonetheless, was not founded upon Truth. Continuing, the former Hebrew of Hebrews and Pharisee of Pharisees said,

> *For not knowing about God's righteousness, and seeking to es-*
> *tablish THEIR OWN, they did not subject themselves to the*
> *righteousness of God. For Christ is the end of the law for righ-*
> *teousness to everyone who believes. (vv. 3,4)*

How profound and profoundly apropos the issue Paul ad-
dresses here is to the matter of idolatrous false teaching in that
he specifically juxtaposes *"zeal for God"* against *"the righteousness of*
God," which actually is referring to "rightstanding with God," or
in other words how one obtains rightstanding with God.

When Jesus of Nazareth at the age of thirty was revealed as
and took on the role of the Christ, He truly became *"THE* (only)
Way [to God], *THE* (only) *Truth* [all spiritual truth, wisdom, and
understanding), *and THE* (only) [Eternal] *Life* [in communion and
fellowship with God]*"* (Jn. 14:6). From the moment Jesus was revealed as the Christ, the Messiah, the Door into fellowship with
the Father, from that very moment, Judaism and the Old Covenant (not to be confused with the Old Testament books of the
Bible) were made obsolete. That is to say that from the moment
the Christ was manifested, faith in Christ became the ONLY
means to attaining rightstanding with God. The absolution of
our sins through Jesus' shed blood became the NEW Covenant,
the *"new and living way"* (Heb. 10:20) by which those who believed
in Him were granted free and equal access unto and communion
with God.

From then on, the Old Covenant, wherein rightstanding with
God was attained by strict adherence to the ordinances of the
Mosaic Law, was no longer in effect. Thus, the statement: *"Christ is*
*the end of the law **for righteousness** to everyone who believes"* (Rom.
10:4). Christ's manifestation meant the end of the law in regard
to obtaining righteousness, or rightstanding, with God through
it. Now, *"everyone who BELIEVES"* has rightstanding with God, *"by*
grace... through faith" (Eph. 2:8).

The obsolescence of the Old Covenant and its replacement
by the New Covenant does not mean, however, as some ignorantly
surmise, that the Truth God revealed in the writings comprising
the books of the Old Testament section of the Bible are now null
and void. It was not God or His Truth that changed between the
Old Covenant era and the New Covenant era, but rather only
the WAY we get to God, that is, the way of attaining unto
rightstanding with God.

I always find it fascinating and more than a little ironic that in the very last Old Testament Book, Malachi, God resoundingly declares: *"For I am the Lord, I change not."* (Mal. 3:6, KJV). I think the Lord strategically planted that statement in that Book for the very purpose of debunking all the religious theorists' claims that somehow He changed between the Old and New Covenants. He did not. As the verse implies, He cannot change, because He is the Sovereign and Perfectly Holy Lord. If God were to change His Nature, which is what He is, which is in turn His Word, He could not be God, for mutability signifies prior imperfection. Yet, He is perfectly perfect, and He is the same yesterday, today, and forever, without any *"shadow of turning."*

Because of the perfection and immutability of the Divine Nature, what God said in the Old Testament writings is just as true and trustworthy now in the New Testament age. *"Not one word of ALL his good promises have ever failed"*—whether they are in New or Old Testament writings, and regardless of what era He said it in. I unabashedly repeat that the only thing that has changed between the Old Testament and the New is the WAY by which we attain rightstanding with God. Otherwise, what He said and established in the Old Testament is still true in the New Testament dispensation.

If *anything* God said or established in the Old Testament were to have changed, He surely would have told us. Generally speaking, however, God is not given to superfluity. Redundancy is not a requirement in the realm of God, which is to say that it is not mandatory that God reiterate in the New Testament writings something He said in the Old Testament writings in order for it to be effectual in the New Testament Age. Anything He has ever said is **forever** settled in Heaven; it is immutable Divine Law, unless He changes it, and when He changes something He publishes that change brazenly and unequivocally. And, the implications and applications of this irrefutable assertion are great in a number of important areas of doctrine under debate and in dispute today in which mere human opinion and religious bias and tradition are being exalted by some above the revealed knowledge of God.

Getting back to the main point inherent in the Apostle Paul's allusion to the Jews' *"zeal without knowledge,"* he said, *"not knowing about GOD'S righteousness,"* that is to say, the way God had established for the attaining of rightstanding with Him, which is through faith in Jesus the Messiah, not knowing about that, the Jews sought *"to establish THEIR OWN,"* and *"they did not subject themselves to the righteousness of God."* Now this is the ultimate problem with the idolatry of false teaching and indeed every kind of idolatry—it replaces God's method for gaining rightstanding with Him, which method is clearly revealed in His Word, with a contrived and incongruous doctrine that has been fashioned and formed in someone's own human mind. Not knowing about God's righteousness, and not wanting to subject themselves to the specific requisites of God's righteousness, they seek to establish their own. That is precisely what all idolatry is: substituting a false gospel for the true, a false *religion* for God's method for *righteousness*, a false god for the One and Only True God, making a god out of one's own religious thoughts and contrived religious methodologies. It is genuine zeal for wanting to attain unto Godlikeness, but on one's own terms, without whole surrender and submission unto God Himself and the Way He has established for attainment of that very status.

It is, I understand, difficult to think of zeal as being anything other than a most commendable and desirable trait. But, not always! In fact, there are case stories in the Bible that illustrate very vividly that misplaced zeal can be quite deadly! A prime example is that of King David who with great zealousness for God in attempting to accomplish the extremely noble and virtuous goal of retrieving the Ark of the Covenant and returning it to its proper place of veneration caused one of his most loyal and beloved servants, Uzza, to be struck down dead by God Himself in an outburst of holy wrath, all because David violated certain particulars of God's established ordinance regarding the method for transportation of the Ark. David was full of zeal, and his zeal was not for some worldly or self-aggrandizing achievement, but for THE THINGS OF GOD! Nevertheless, his misdirected zeal got a beloved friend killed and invoked the wrath of God, despite all the pageantry, and pomp and circumstance, as David along with all of Israel were praising and *"celebrating before God with all their might, even with songs and with lyres, harps, tambourines, cymbals, and with trumpets"* (1 Chron. 13:8).

God tells us that the real life incidences that occurred in Old Testament days *"happened to them as an example and they were written for our instruction, upon whom the ends of the ages have come"*

(1 Cor. 10:11). The poignant moral of this story to all of us living at *"the ends of the ages"* is that as needful and desirable as the fervency of zeal is, zeal, no matter how fervent and fiery, cannot and will not ever supersede the necessity of obedience to God's already established Word, Will, and Ways, that is, His ordinances and order. Even all that we do for and as an offering unto God must be done or offered up according to the ordinances, according to *His* Word, Will, and Way. We cannot do it our own way, and be operating in the favor and approval of God. Neither can we seek and serve Him according to our own doctrines and ideas for seeking and serving Him, and be under his favor and approval. When the fleeting vapor that is our natural life is over, and we stand before the Righteous Judge to be judged on the basis of our deeds (Rom. 2:6, et al.), faithfulness and obedience to Him will be the standard, not how emotionally incited, fervent, or zealous we were.

Zeal never overrides or negates the necessity for obedience of the specific requisites of God's order and ordinances. Indeed, this is the import of the Spirit's admonition conveyed through the Apostle Paul as a final exhortation at the culmination of a dissertation in which he urges believers to employ the manifestations of the Spirit, "But let all things (spiritual ministrations) be done decently and in order" (1 Cor. 14:40). So, bottom line is: it's either GOD'S Way, or NO way!

CHAPTER EIGHT
ULTIMATE ACCOUNTABILITY

Y ou see, when taken to their fullest extent, these fallacious and false teachings and the "spiritual covering" aspect in particular, culminate in an infringement upon the Biblical fact of ultimate personal accountability to God, which is to say that in the end every person is accountable to God, and to God alone, for his conduct and for the substance of the life he or she lived. Ultimately, it is to an Almighty and All-knowing God, that we must give account for the totality of our lives. Ultimately each believer is accountable only to the authority of God, and not to any alleged authority of men.

This Truth and its veracity is unequivocally and wholly supported by the preponderance of Scripture, and proof-texts corroborating this absolute fact are so numerous that to quote them all would require a separate volume of its own. But, there is one passage that states it about as directly and succinctly as it can be stated, which is, Romans 14:12: *"So then EACH OF US shall GIVE ACCOUNT of HIMSELF to GOD."*

Moreover, the verses that precede this particular passage are also extremely enlightening and germane to this point regarding ultimate accountability unto God. In verse four, Paul poses the consummate question to which every believer would be well advised to take careful heed: *"Who are you to judge the servant of another?"*

To judge someone else, it is imperative to understand, by its very nature, means that the person who is sitting in the seat of the judge is of a greater status, standing, authority, and behavioral stature, than the one who is being judged. Yet, clearly an overwhelming preponderance of Scripture teaches that as Jesus stated, *"You* (all believers) *are all on the same level as brothers"* (Mat. 23:8, L.B., parenthesis added by author). As established repeatedly throughout this book, in the Kingdom of God there is absolute parity among believers. There is no such a thing as "big me, little you" in the Kingdom of God. Oh, to be sure, in real life, demonstration of carnal attitudes of ascendancy and arrogance over fellows is just as common among purporting believers as it is in the world. But, that is not the way it really is in the Kingdom of God and from God's perspective. Such fleshly attitudes are of the category of the *"evil passions and desires"* that every believer must crucify if he is going to show forth evidence or fruit that he has been genuinely Born Again and been made a bona fide partaker of the attributes of the Divine Nature (Gal. 5:24; 2 Pet. 2:4).

Notice also in the verse cited (Rom. 14:4) the phrase *"servant of another."* This makes it abundantly clear that every believer is a servant of God, not of any man. Even when of our own volition we lay down our lives to serve others, we do so because the Person we are serving ultimately in so doing is God, not even the people we are serving, though they are the ostensible recipients of our service. The verse continues by saying: *"To HIS OWN MASTER he stands or falls; and stand he will, for THE LORD is able to make him stand."* In saying, *"THE LORD is able to make him stand,"* the passage identifies the *"master"* of the believer as being the Lord Jesus Himself, and not any human.

Verses seven through nine of the same chapter in Romans go on to clearly indicate that every believer "belongs" ultimately to the Lord, and thus is not the subject of any human being in terms of ultimate accountability for his or her life:

> *For not one of us lives for himself, and not one dies for himself; for if we live, we live FOR THE LORD, or if we die, we die FOR THE LORD; therefore whether we live or die, WE ARE THE LORD'S. For to this end Christ died and lived, that HE might be LORD both of the dead and of the living.*

But, the next verse, verse ten, really puts it all into proper perspective by reminding us that none of us have the right to take unto ourselves the status of judge over our fellows with regard to the final analysis, assessment, and adjudication of their lives, as well as the fact that none of us have attained unto the transcendent or elite status required to grant us the right to regard a fellow believer with contempt or condescension, or regard any fellow believer, who is also a joint-heir, that is, equal-heir, with Christ, as in any way inferior or "subjectable" to us so as to be their judges, because we are not the *judges*; rather, we all are the *"judgees,"* being judged ourselves by *"the righteous Judge"* (2 Tim. 4:8):

> *But you, why do you judge your brother? Or you again, why do you regard your brother with contempt? FOR WE SHALL ALL STAND BEFORE THE JUDGMENT SEAT OF GOD. (Rom. 14:10)*

Hebrews 12:23 refers to *"THE Judge of ALL,"* which is none other than God Himself. Hebrews 10:30 plainly tells us: *"THE LORD will judge His people,"* which means that ultimate accounting and the final adjudication of our lives is relegated to the Lord alone. The reason for this is simple: perfect and perfectly righteous and just judgment requires omniscience and infinite knowledge and wisdom, which we, in our human estate of extremely finite knowledge, do not possess. Only God is capable of judging *"the thoughts and intentions of the heart"* with perfect knowledge, wisdom, and understanding, for it is to His eyes, the manifold eyes of the Spirit, **alone** that all that we are is *"open and laid bare"* (Heb. 4:12,13). Only He who knows us most can judge us best. No one knows us, who we really are, the totality of our constitution and the reasons behind it, like God knows us.

Thus, we see the incontrovertible and unequivocal truth that ultimately every believer is accountable to God and not to any mere mortal. As I have said elsewhere in this volume, only the one with the nail prints in His hands is the one who has earned the right to be our Lord, Master, and Savior. This is precisely the import of James' statement wherein speaking of Jesus He says: *"There is ONLY ONE Lawgiver and Judge, THE ONE WHO IS ABLE TO SAVE and to destroy, but who are you to judge your neighbor?"* (Jas. 4:12).

So, dear saint of God, the next time someone tries to "pull rank" on you, intimidate, or subjugate you with some humanly contrived, illegitimate, invalid, and non-existent ilk of pseudo-authority, ask that person to stretch forth his or her hands, and look to see if there are nail-holes in those hands. If not, just have a little chuckle within yourself, turn, and walk away, and forget it! Because that person ain't *your* Lord or *your* Master! He's just another pretender and imposter motivated by an Antichrist spirit! Praise **Jesus**, the One who is able to save and destroy to the uttermost, forever! He alone is Lord!

CHAPTER NINE
THE CHIEF SHEPHERD OF GOD'S FLOCK

What all of this speaks to us and what all ministers need to be reminded of from time to time is that for as much power and legitimate authority (accompanied with the attendant responsibility) Jesus has vested in us as His "standins," His under-shepherds, to minister unto the Flock of God on His behalf, notwithstanding, and without any equivocation—it is Jesus Christ **Himself**, the King of Kings, and Lord of Lords, who is the TRUE and SUPREME SHEPHERD. All of the rest of us are not even worthy, compared to Him, to be called after His name or to bear in any degree the title of which He alone has proved Himself so inimitably worthy—*"Good Shepherd."* Those mere under-shepherds on Earth who are so overtly impressed by themselves and their own "accomplishments" would certainly do well to take a cue in humility from the Twenty-Four Chief Elders who, when face to face with *"the One who was sitting on the Throne,"* did *"**cast down their crowns before the Throne**, saying, 'Worthy art THOU, O LORD, to receive glory and honor and power.'"*

Compared to the glory of the SUPREME SHEPHERD, we are poor and miserable substitutes, mere mortals of flesh and bone, with no worthiness of our own, nothing with which to commend us to God, or in reality even to our own fellows. It is only as we reflect His Image, His glory, His Light, which we do only ever so sporadically and imperfectly, that there is anything comely or of worth within us. We merely reflect, with varying and variable degrees of illumination, unto a lost, broken, downcast, hurting, spiritually bankrupt, and dying world of undone sinners the Image of a glorious and risen Savior who suffered immeasurable shame, disgrace, sorrow, and pain, far beyond anything we could even imagine much less ourselves experience, in order to set the captives free from their bondage and eternal damnation.

It is these sentiments and understanding the Apostle Peter,

who over a period of three and one-half years had walked and talked and eaten and lived with this GREAT SHEPHERD OF OUR SOULS, was trying desperately to convey when he wrote:

> *Therefore, I exhort the elders (Fivefold Ministers) among you, as your fellow elder and witness of the sufferings of Christ, and a partaker also of the glory that is to be revealed, shepherd the flock of God among you, exercising oversight not under compulsion, but voluntarily, according to the will of God; not for sordid gain, but with eagerness; nor yet as lording it over those allotted to your charge, but proving to be examples to the flock. And when the **Chief Shepherd** appears, you will receive the unfading crown of glory. (1 Pet. 5:14, parenthesis added by author)*

The Amplified Bible's version of this passage conveys in even more graphic terms the sense of what the Apostle was communicating in these words:

> *I warn and counsel the elders among you—the pastors and spiritual guides of the church—as a fellow elder and as an eyewitness [called to testify] of the sufferings of Christ, as well as a sharer in the glory (the honor and splendor) that is to be revealed (disclosed, unfolded): **Tend—nurture, guard, guide and fold**—the flock of God that is [your responsibility], not by **coercion** or **constraint** but **willingly**; not **dishonorably motivated** by the **advantages and profits** [belonging to the office] but eagerly and cheerfully. Not (as **arrogant, dictatorial** and **overbearing** persons) **domineering** over those in your charge, but being **examples—patterns and models of Christian living**— to the flock (the congregation). And [then] when the CHIEF SHEPHERD is revealed you will win the conqueror's crown of glory.*

To me personally there are few things as repulsive and reprehensible as a "spiritual" (or, more appropriately, "religious") leader who is all the very things the above text warns us not to be: arrogant, dictatorial, overbearing, and domineering, over the meek and innocent sheep of God's Flock under his charge. This, to me, is about as despicable as it gets—to take advantage of and exploit the need people have for a human pattern and model of Jesus that they can see, and use that need as a pretext to dominate and subjugate those needy people for sordid and self-aggrandizing personal gain. I know that it is also a stench in the nostrils of God! And, if it is so utterly offensive and repulsive to me, one who is of the same fleshly nature as they, it must only be the expansive and encompassing mercy and forbearance of God that keeps Him from wiping such vile violators completely off the face of the Earth and taking them instantly to their final and just reward.

Whose Flock Is It? Whose Sheep Are They?

I mean, it appears to me that when those in leadership positions engage in such sordid attitudes and activity they have forgotten one very vital and important factor in the scenario, which is that the sheep don't belong to any man. The true sheep of God, which is every truly Born Again believer, are all the sheep of GOD'S FLOCK. The true sheep, it will come as a shock to many "leaders," are GOD'S sheep, and Jesus is the true Shepherd of God's Fold. They are not the personal possession and pawns of human pastors, despite the fact that the attitudes of many pastors seem to reflect that they think they are. Human shepherds, it must never be forgotten, are merely *"custodial under-shepherds,"* if you will.

The Apostle Peter made all this abundantly clear in the passage we just examined, where, in verse two, he exhorted the presbytery of the local church to *"shepherd THE FLOCK OF GOD."* Moreover, it is on this foundational fact that he bases his further exhortations to under-shepherds not to lord over the flock, to but rather prove themselves examples, visible models, live representations, of the Good Shepherd that the sheep can actually behold with their physical eyes.

Another passage that specifically alludes to the fact that it is to GOD'S FLOCK that the sheep belong is found in the Apostle Paul's exhortation unto the eldership (Fivefold Ministers) of the church at Ephesus, whom he had called together for a final word of exhortation and admonition prior to his departure to Rome. To these *"episkopos"* (elders, overseers, shepherds) he said:

> Be on guard for yourselves and for all **THE FLOCK**, among which the Holy Spirit has made you **overseers**, to **shepherd** the church **OF GOD** which he purchased with his own blood. (Ac. 20:28)

In this passage we see *"the flock"* equated with *"the church of God."* *"The church of God"* is the *"Ekklesia,"* the assemblage of the "called out" saints Jesus referred to when He said, *"I will build My church; and the gates* (lit., powers) *of Hades shall not overpower it."* In this Truth-replete statement, Jesus was succinctly indicating four major points about this *"Ekklesia"* He was personally engaged in building: one, it was His own personal possession, and no other person or group of persons; two, this particular group of called out, consecrated, and set apart believers, the Holy Race, is the only one He Himself is engaged in establishing; three, those "churches" or collections of peoples being led and built by mere men apart from His personal engagement are imposters and bogus counterfeits, false imitations, of the true Church that He Himself is building; and four, that the identifying and distinguishing mark of the true Church that Jesus Himself is building is that the individuals of this Ekklesia, and thus its collective whole as well, are not being overpowered and vanquished in terms of constitution, character, and conduct, by the powers and assailment of the devil's kingdom, i.e., *"Hades."*

Relating all this with what Paul said to the elders of the church at Ephesus: the bona fide, Born Again, called out, set apart from the world, sanctified, consecrated believers who comprise this Ekklesia that Jesus is building, are the exclusive possession of Christ Himself; they are the sheep of the Good Shepherd, Jesus; they are the sheep of God's Flock, and not that of any mere human. The true sheep, the sheep of this Ekklesia, are those who *"belong to Christ,"* meaning they are His possession, and are those who *"have crucified the flesh with its* (carnal and worldly and devilish) *passions and desires"* (Gal. 5:24, parenthesis added by author), which speaks of their having been sanctified and set apart in deed, not merely metaphorically.

CHAPTER TEN
ANTICHRIST WOLVES

Now the portion of the Apostle Paul's poignant and impassioned exhortation to the Ephesian elders just quoted began with an admonition to *"Be on guard for yourselves and for all the flock...."* The subsequent verses specify what it was that the Apostle told them it was their responsibility from God as shepherds and overseers of God's flock to guard against—the intrusion and infusion of *"savage wolves."* He indicated this was an inevitable occurrence following his departure unto Rome (where he would be put to death), inevitable, presumably, that is, if preclusive action was not taken.

Though Paul himself was speaking entirely of the churches of that day to whom he had ministerial responsibility, his Spirit-inspired admonition, especially since it is now part of canonized Scripture, is also a dire and rousing exhortation to the Ekklesia of Christ of every era, including the present one. Here is the entire text:

> *Be on guard for yourselves and for all the flock, among which the Holy Spirit has made you overseers, to shepherd the church of God which he purchased with his own blood. I know that after my departure* **SAVAGE WOLVES will come in among you, not sparing the flock; and from among your own selves men will arise, speaking perverse things, to draw away the disciples after them.** *Therefore be on the alert, remembering that night and day for a period of three years I did not cease to admonish each one with tears. (Ac. 20:28)*

Paul was warning these Fivefold ministers who were charged with edificational and governmental responsibility that there would be persons purporting to be anointed and appointed leaders infiltrating their ranks who were false, self-imposed interlopers motivated by self-aggrandizement, who would exploit the sheep for their own personal sordid gain. Paul seemed to be indicating that some of these *"ravenous wolves in sheep's clothing,"* as Jesus called them, would emerge even out of this very group of current elders who were assembled before him. He said these imposters would teach perverted, erroneous, and unproven doctrines in order to draw away the disciples after *themselves*, in effect causing those disciples to fall away from *Jesus* as their Shepherd in order to follow after and adhere to these errant and bogus ministers.

Now in so deceiving and leading astray those sheep, these seducers would prove they are "Antichrist wolves," possessed and driven by an evil Antichrist spirit of the devil, because they are actually engaged in seducing the sheep to abandon Christ and the Truth in order to follow after these false shepherds and false saviors and their fallacious doctrines and indoctrinations.

This is precisely what is transpiring in the case of the perverted and invalid Discipleship/Shepherding doctrines and those who propagate them. Nothing could be a more exact fulfillment of what the Apostle Paul predicted would transpire than the overt abuses and excesses in terms of human shepherding taking place today in groups and churches under the auspices of these fallacious doctrines. Those teaching and operating in accordance with these deviant doctrines are indeed *"drawing away disciples after themselves"* and away from Jesus as their true Shepherd and Savior, abrogating Him in those offices, and substituting themselves instead.

Discipleship shepherds via the tenets of these errant doctrines pose and interpose themselves as the de facto shepherd and savior of their followers, even though they may profusely evoke the name of Jesus in all their public discourse. By *"speaking perverse things,"* these *"savage wolves,"* motivated by sordid and demonic passions and desires for ascendency, adulation, and personal aggrandizement, have set themselves in the place of veneration Christ alone is worthy to occupy. Such usurpation is overtly and quintessentially Antichrist.

CHAPTER ELEVEN
COMPLETENESS IN CHRIST

A s I begin to bring the examination of this inane notion of "spiritual covering" provided by mere human shepherds to a culmination, I want to make one final important point related to the focus of this chapter that further establishes the complete absurdity of this notion. It has to do with the individual believer's *completeness in Christ.*

In his letter to the believers at Colossae, the Apostle Paul capsulized his ministry and calling in this statement:

> *And we proclaim Him* (Christ), *admonishing every man and teaching every man with all wisdom, that we may present every man* **complete in Christ**. *(Col. 1:28)*

Though his intent was to summarize his own ministry and calling, his statement has afforded us a succinct synopsis of what the ministry per se is about. All of the elements of valid ministry are represented in the verbiage of this verse. The primary function of all ministry is to: *proclaim* (preach) **Christ** as Lord, Master, and Savior of all, juxtaposed to human lords, masters, and saviors; *admonish* (warn) **every human being** of the perils and consequences of disregard and disobedience of God and His Master Plan; *teaching* **every human being** of the principles of the Kingdom of God (i.e., the authority of Christ [Rev. 12:10]); and, to *present* **every human being** (who will give heed to what we minister to them) back to God **complete in Christ**.

The ultimate goal of all ministry is to make everyone who has submitted to the gospel of the authority of Christ over his/her life totally *"complete in Christ,"* which is to say, spiritually **whole**; which is to say, **holy**. This is the ultimate mission of all true ministry and every true minister, to make everyone to whom they minister spiritually complete in Christ.

Conversely, whether those who subscribe to and engage in

them realize it or not, and I am sure there are some who genuinely do not realize it, Discipleship/Shepherding doctrines and practices by their very nature do not promote the complete dependence on Christ that produces spiritual completion in Christ. Rather, as already discussed, the disposition of these doctrines are decidedly Antichrist in that they teach adherents to place their faith, hope, trust, confidence, and essentially their destiny in the spiritual efficacy of their human leaders, who, the heresy purports, are their effectual mediators unto God. Simply put, Shepherding followers are taught to place all of their faith in their leaders, rather than looking through them to see Christ Himself as Lord and Savior.

As we shall discuss in the next chapter, those who have been genuinely anointed and appointed by Jesus to Fivefold Ministry offices certainly have a very valid and important role with regard to the spiritual edification of individual believers as well as the collective Church. However, Fivefold Ministers are like the moon to the sun, they have no glory or light of their own, but merely reflect *"the True Light which, coming into the world, enlightens every man"* who believes in the Light (Jn. 1:9). Like John the Baptist, Fivefold Ministers are not themselves the light, but rather merely *"bear witness of the Light, that all might believe* [in the True Light] *through (them)"* (v. 7). Ministers are not the source of the Light, they merely reflect and impart unto others the Light and Life of Christ through the *proclaiming* aspect of their ministry, that is, the revelation of Christ via preaching and teaching, coupled with the *portraying* aspect of their ministry, which is the revelation of Christ via their own exemplary conduct after the pattern of Christ.

It is by the True Light, Christ Himself, shining on us and in us that the darkness of sin is dispelled and vanquished by the Light of God's Nature. Only Christ, the True Light Itself, the source of the Light, can do that. And, it is this, and this alone that makes us *"complete."* Thus, our spiritual completeness can only be *"in Christ."* But, in Christ, we are indeed complete. And, so absolute and perfect is this condition of *"complete"* that it is intrinsically impossible to improve upon it. Complete is complete. You cannot be more complete than complete.

Hence, when it is all said and done the only role that any human being has played in that completion that is attained "in

Christ" is that of merely being a reflector of the glory of the Light, and even that is at best sporadic and imperfect, hindered as it is by the voids of darkness remaining yet within us all. Make no mistake about it—all the glory belongs exclusively to the Light, not the imperfect reflectors of the Light.

Let us all therefore resolve to ascribe all glory to the One to whom it belongs, claiming none for ourselves, thereby sparing ourselves the eternal embarrassment and shame that will otherwise be ours when finally we stand before the Throne of the Light and witness firsthand the blinding brilliance of His Glory, which shall reveal our utter inanity, insanity, and hubris of having supposed that we ourselves were anything other than a mere reflector of the Light.

CHAPTER TWELVE
THE FIFTEEN "RS" OF RECOVERY FROM AUTHORITARIAN ABUSE

Everything written in this book prior to this last chapter has been dedicated to the purpose of identifying erroneous hyper-authoritarian doctrines and practices being espoused and implemented within Charismatic and other Neo-Pentecostal churches and groups. But, certainly, a work such as this would be wholly incomplete and deficient if it did not include instruction regarding how those caught up in the throes of such "charismatic captivation" can be set free and recover from it. This final chapter is devoted to that end.

Over nearly the entire course of my ministry, I have been studying this matter of hyper-authoritarianism, weighing it against Scripture, and ministering in various ways to many victims of authoritarian exploitation and abuse. Based on my experience and the understanding attained during that time, I have concluded there are fifteen primary actions that victims must take in order to break the fetters of predomination binding them and effect a full recovery from all the spiritual and psychological effects they have experienced. Though it is generally prudent to avoid improper dogmatism, there are some matters that require definitive actions in order to achieve a designated result. This, I believe, is one of those matters. Though I believe the steps I proffer here are critical and imperative, I would certainly allow that there could be other actions required to recover from authoritarian exploitation that I have not delineated. However, the ones I *have* enumerated here, I believe are absolutely necessary if effectual and comprehensive recovery is to be realized.

Although the effects of authoritarian abuse are profound, the actions necessary to break its bondage and to bring recovery are comparatively simple; not simplistic, perhaps, but simple. Thus, I have presented them in as simple and straightforward terms as I know how to present them, not only because of their simplicity, but also in order to make them as understandable as possible. Please note that the book I am referring to is *Charismatic Captivation*, of which this chapter originally was a part.

1. Read—*this book and The Book.*

By no means is this a promotional gimmick to sell books. Though I may not be unbiased in this assessment and to some it will seem presumptuous if not hubristic, I am fully persuaded that God inspired and commissioned the writing of this book rather than it being the product of mere human invention. Because its premise is founded so squarely upon the Word of God and the assertions made within it are corroborated by myriad Scripture quotations, this volume contains Truth and thus the effectual anointing to set captives free from the fetters of religious captivation. Jesus said, *"If you abide in My Word, then are you truly disciples of Mine; and you shall know the TRUTH, and the TRUTH will make you free!"*

2. Receive—*the teaching and reproof in this book.*

Many times people *read* books and materials, but they never really *"receive"* the information and impartation inherent in the material they read. This is especially true when it comes to teaching that involves correction and reproof, because our natural tendency is to *reject* that which is essentially saying we have been wrong in some respect. Indeed, *receiving* is not automatic when one *reads* something; rather, one must make a deliberate effort to *receive* what he or she *reads.* When you read this book along with the Word of God for validation, be sure that you are indeed *receiving* into your spirit and mind what you are *reading,* and allow the Lord to *regenerate* you spiritually with the washing of the Word.

3. Renew—*your mind regarding the relevant concepts.*

Read and meditate upon this book and the Bible in order to **renew** your mind regarding the concepts upon which these erroneous teachings and practices are based. *"As a man thinketh in his heart, so IS he"* (Pro. 23:7)—thus, we are what we **think.** So, it is absolutely essential that we **renew** our minds, that is, our thinking, to be in accord with the Word of God, which is the "thinking" of God. In this case, the overall essential truth one must understand is that *"where the Spirit of the Lord is, there is **liberty** (2 Cor.

3:17)," not bondage of any kind, nature, or degree. *"He whom the Son sets free, is free indeed!"* (Jn. 8:36). **Anything** that brings people into bondage, especially bondage to men, is patently NOT OF GOD!

4. *Recognize—these doctrines and practices are error.*

To truly be set free from the bondage resulting from the hyper-authoritarian doctrines and practices addressed in this volume, it is absolutely imperative that you recognize that they are not merely, "a little off-base," but rather that they are patently false, erroneous, errant, unscriptural, and heretical. Any teaching or hypothesis is either truth or it is error; there is no in-between. Even a mixture of truth and error is error. It is the minute3, undetectable quantity of poison on the steak that kills the guarddog, allowing the thief entry. This is the modus operandi of the master-thief, Satan, who comes with a big, succulent filet mignon steak of truth that he has corrupted with a tiny, nearly imperceptible smidgeon of error. He lures with Truth and kills with the error.

5. *Recant and Renounce—all associated false teaching and thinking.*

I have found over and over again, in ministering to victims of false teaching that it is essential that once they realize the teaching they have been indoctrinated with is false, they also take the next step of actually recanting and renouncing those doctrines. This is accomplished simply by literally making an oral statement to the effect of: "I recant and renounce the false and demonically-inspired doctrines and practices of....(in this case the Discipleship/Shepherding doctrines and practices)." The Bible indicates people can be snared by their own words spoken out of their own mouth (Pro. 6:2). I believe this is what happens when we accept and speak the concepts of false doctrine. So, to reverse the effects of these doctrines, we must recant and renounce the words we have uttered in expressing those concepts.

6. *Repent—from all associated and indicated sin.*

Once the truths and perspectives presented in this book are understood and embraced, it becomes incontrovertibly clear that these hyper-authoritarian doctrines and practices are founded in sin, i.e., rebellious and ungodly attitudes. Those who have been, especially proactive, participants in these doctrines need to candidly search their heart and allow the Holy Spirit to put His finger on the character flaws that caused them to be attracted to these doctrines and practices, "fall out of agreement with them" (cf., Amos 3:3), making a definitive "mind-change" as to the "rightness" of these doctrines and practices, and then "turn away" or "repent" from them in simple and sincere confession to the Lord.

7. *Request—forgiveness, from God and people.*

Once you realize you have been a participant in unscriptural doctrines and ungodly practices, forgiveness is needed and should, of course, be desired. First, one should request forgiveness from God for having departed from the paths of righteousness. Secondly, you will also need to seek forgiveness from the people you have personally involved or affected as a result of your espousal and/or propagation of these fallacious doctrines and participation in these sinful practices. Whether you were a "leader" at some level in one of these authoritarian systems or merely one of the "led," there are people whose lives you have somehow effected with what you believed at the time to be "truth." Now that you realize you were under deception, you will need to go to those persons to whom the Holy Spirit leads you, confess to them you now realize you were wrong, and ask them to forgive you. The Holy Spirit is really the only One who can make it plain to you those to whom you need to go; and He *will*, when you seek Him in all sincerity, humility, and honesty.

8. *Realize—you've been a participant in erroneous teaching and practices, thereby subjecting yourself to demonic influence and bondage.*

It is important that you actually come to the realization without any "fudging," rationalizing, euphemizing, or justifying that you have been a participant in a system of false teaching and unscriptural practices that are centered in witchcraft and inspired by demons, and that as a result you have subjected yourself to at least the potential of demonic influence and bondage. This may seem rudimentary to some, but my experience in dealing with demonic incursion demonstrates it is nonetheless a critical step in the process of release and recovery that cannot be avoided or circumvented. It is important to face this possibility of demonic incursion head-on and forthrightly.

9. Reach—out for deliverance.

Throughout the course of this book, I have indicated my conviction, which has been corroborated by a preponderance of extensive experience, that falling prey to deception predicated on *"doctrines of demons"* and *"deceiving spirits"* frequently incurs demonic incursion of some sort and degree into the life of the victim. It follows then, if this is indeed true, as my experience and basic spiritual "sense" tells me it is, that those who have been participants in these doctrines and practices need to **reach** out for deliverance to someone who believes in and ministers deliverance. Of course and unfortunately, not all pastors believe in deliverance and that a bona fide believer could be subjected to demonic influence, despite the preponderance of Biblical proof that exists. Obviously, I cannot debate that issue here, however, I have authored and published a manual that deals with the matter of deliverance from demonic power that may be obtained by contacting our ministry office. But, in almost every geographical region, God has stationed *someone* who ministers deliverance, who in some cases are not conventional "pastors" in conventional churches, but who may have John-the-Baptist-type ministries in the wilderness, and who may be regarded by the "mainstream" ministers as spiritual "desert rats." If not, He certainly will send an itinerant minister to an area where people are in need of deliverance, in response to the earnest petitions of praying saints. Regardless who it is God uses, most victims will need to receive some deliverance ministry, and would be well-advised to seek it. I always say if there are no demons in there, it won't hurt a thing to command them to come out. No harm, no foul! Moreover, it's a complete waste of time to wrangle about "where" the demons are—in your spirit (which they can't be in a bona fide Born-Again believer, unless he or she has fallen away), your soul (i.e., mind, will, and emotions), or your body—rather, as I always say, if they are in your HIP-POCKET, they need to be driven out!

10. Release—all "covenantees."

In order to experience true liberation from all the effects, ramifications, and consequences of involvement in these enslavement systems, which are rooted in witchcraft/sorcery, it is imperative that you release yourself from all "covenants" of men in which you have been involved. This means covenants or contracts you have made with leaders to whom you have pledged submission and support, as well as those with people who may be in any form of "submission" to you. This will require that you comprehend and be convinced of the fallacy and invalidity of such "covenants," as delineated in this book, otherwise the strong indoctrination you have received regarding the sacrosanctity of them will continue to hold you in bondage to the human leaders to whom you have submitted yourself. It is true that God wants us to follow through on vows we have made, however, only legitimate and Scripturally authorized vows, which these are not. These "covenants" and contracts are totally invalidated by the Word of God, and therefore not recognized by God. Thus, to break and negate them, not only is approved but even required by God, and to do so is *obedience*, not *disobedience*, to God.

11. Reflect—*on the methods, mechanisms, motives, and message of the group of which you've been a member.*

Once you have assimilated the information in this book, it is necessary that you evaluate and assess the methods, mechanisms, motives, and overall message of the ministry of which you have been a part. Now this will be difficult to do because you have been thoroughly indoctrinated with the idea that to engage in such critical scrutiny is being rebellious, indicative of a "critical spirit," and that it is unauthorized "judgment." But, you need to allow yourself to accept the absolute fact that that is a LIE!

The Bereans were attributed by the Holy Spirit as being *"noble-minded"* for having thoroughly scrutinized the teaching of the apostles against Scripture to prove its validity (Ac. 17:11). The meticulous Doctor Luke wrote his synopsis only after having *"investigated everything carefully* [thoroughly]*"* (Lk. 1:3). The Holy Spirit also instructed us to *"examine everything carefully; hold fast to that which is good; abstain from every form of evil"* (1 Thes. 5:21,22). Moreover, we are outright commanded by the Holy Spirit to *"investigate and search out and inquire thoroughly"* any teaching or doctrine especially which is suspected of leading people away from the absolute and exclusive Lordship of Christ (Deut. 13:14).

But, above all this, Jesus taught us that we will be able to *"know"* a *tree*, metaphorically speaking, whether an individual or a ministry, with respect to its goodness (God-likeness) and validity, by the nature of the fruit it produces, which means that we are required to be "fruit inspectors" of both ministers and ministries.

Such scrutiny, investigation, examination, assessment, is "AUTHO-RIZED judgment!" and is an absolute necessity! So, understand you are not doing *wrong* when you are engaging in it, but *right!*

12. Run—from that church-group and relationships with those who espouse and employ these teachings and practices.

In this day of "positive thinking" and "overcoming attitudes" it is difficult for many people to accept the concept that there are some situations that can only be "overcome" by putting it in "B" for boogie, and running like a scalded rabbit. Typically, those who realize that their church-group has been caught up in deception, feel what in actuality is a "false burden" to get their friends, the collective group, and even the leadership to "see" what they now see and to bring change to the group. But, the truth of the matter, unfortunately, is that that never happens. Usually, people are exactly where the "want" to be, both in terms of their spiritual beliefs and participations, as well as the church they attend, and most people do not at all respond favorably when the validity or veracity of either of those are challenged. Consequently, most "departees" will have to leave on their own and alone, despite the tendency toward the need to take others with them as a psychological means of validating their conclusions, decisions, and actions.

13. Realign—yourself with a church-group and friends who do not espouse these teachings and practices.

Once you have separated yourself from the church-group of which you were a part, it is important that you eventually realign yourself with a new church-group and friends who do not espouse and employ these heretical doctrines and practices. Some people find it necessary to take some time out from such intense and all-consuming church involvement for a period of time in order to clear their minds and gain a different, more balanced perspective of the proper role of a church and a church family. Both of these are important, but not to the detriment or substitution of our direct, personal relationship with the Lord Himself. Some people have gotten so caught up in the mysticism of "Charismania" that, to coin a modern saying, they need to "get a life!" And, it is perfectly okay if you feel that you need to give yourself a little break from constant church-going and involvement, especially if it has become bondage to you. We ARE the Church; you don't have to GO TO a church to be a part of THE church. Rather, we are baptized by the regeneration of the Spirit at the New Birth into the Church (1 Cor. 12:13). Church is not an organization, or a building, or some place you GO TO; rather, it is something believers simply ARE! We are now the Temple, the building of God (1 Cor. 3:9; 2 Cor. 5:1; Eph. 2:21) Yet, it is good to be a part of a brotherhood of believers to whom to relate and from whom we can draw spiritual strength and support. Indeed, that is what "church" is supposed to be. Beware when it becomes or is presented as being more than that. Beware that you not become guilty, by and by, in worshipping the *Church of God* rather than the *God of the Church.*

14. Rest—in God's grace, forgiveness, love, and acceptance.

Once you have taken all the preceding steps, it is vital that you then just REST in God's undeserved favor (grace), His free-flowing forgiveness, His unconditional agape-love, and His complete acceptance. These are the attributes of God, and they are the attributes that distinguish the Divine Nature from human nature. Humans are never as liberal with these as is God, and it is vain to expect them to be. Nevertheless, we can indeed rest in all these, if we will only allow ourselves, though the concept of entering into the Sabbath rest of faith is something participants in these sorts of spiritual societies and systems that are so saturated in "works" will have to learn all over again, if indeed they had ever learned it in the first place.

15. Recommend—this book to other victims of authoritarian abuse.

Once again, this final "R" is, by no means, merely a marketing ploy to sell books. Rather, it is absolutely vital that those who have been victims of religious hyper-authoritarian exploitation and abuse assimilate the information proffered in this volume in order to be set free from the strong delusion and bondage they are under. This is the only book I am aware of dealing effectively and specifically with this matter of authoritarian abuse in the Pentecostal context in particular and possessing the information required to truly set the captives free. There are some books addressing the problem that are written by non-Charismatic and in most cases, anti-Charismatic psychologists or sociologists, however, those I have read, in my opinion, proffer "answers" based in psychology rather than viable and Scriptural spirituality. Most of them also have a blatantly anti-Charismatic slant, and seem to use the existence of these errant and aberrant practices as proof and a pretext for debunking Charismatic theology and discrediting Charismatics and the Charismatic church. This assessment and caveat having been rendered, I have compiled a bibliography dealing with the subject of authoritarian abuse that is available on my ministry website at: slm.org. If you've been affected by spiritual abuse, please visit my deliverance counseling website: DeliveranceNow.com.

As I have reiterated repeatedly throughout this volume *(Charismatic Captivation)* in many ways, I myself am a bona fide Charismatic and am wholly persuaded of the validity of the Charismatic Movement and its Divine orchestration. By no means am I engaging in any form or degree of Charismatic-bashing in this book, but rather proffering what I am fully convinced is valid and very much needed God-inspired reproof and correction of patently unscriptural doctrines and practices that unfortunately are being practiced within much of the Charismatic and Neo-Pentecostal Church.

I am also quite aware that these doctrines and practices are being espoused and employed in other segments and streams of the Church of Jesus as well; however, it is of the Neo-Pentecostal that I am a part, and as such, have a particular "right" to confront concerning needed reproofs. It is my deepest desire and heartfelt prayer that all those who name themselves among the Brotherhood of Christ will give heed to the reproof and admonitions presented in this book, and take the actions necessary to liberate the Children of God from the oppressive captivation of men, for we are called to be **SONS** of God, not **SLAVES** of men. *"He whom the Son sets free, is free indeed!"*

* * * *

Thanks for reading or listening to this book. My trust and prayer is that it has been a blessing to you. I again urge you to read the book from which this book is adapted, *Charismatic Captivation,* which is available from book sellers worldwide and at: RealTruthPublications.com.

ABOUT THE AUTHOR

DR. STEVEN LAMBERT has been ministering the Gospel of Jesus Christ as an ordained minister since 1976, serving as a pastor, prophet, teacher, adjunct professor, radio broadcaster, and a Christian counselor. He is a Doctoral Diplomate Certified Christian Therapist, and holds several earned theological degrees. He also ministers as an apostolic prophet to help establish and strengthen existing churches and plant new ones.

He also serves as the Overseer of *Ephesians Four Network of Churches & Ministers* (ephesiansfour.net), an international fellowship of Fivefold Ministers relating and co-laboring for common purposes, and its subsidiary, *Ephesians Four Network of Deliverance Counselors* (efndc.ephesiansfour.net).

Dr. Lambert is the author/narrator of an ever-increasing number of books, audiobooks, booklets, courses, and other teaching materials (catalog at: realtruthpublications.com), as well as the publisher of an online magazine, *Spirit Life Magazine* (spiritlifemag.com), which is dedicated to extolling, elucidating, and experiencing Life in the Spirit.

Dr. Lambert speaks on the topic of authoritarian abuse and many other vital apostolic/prophetic topics in churches, conferences, and other venues. His bio and scheduling information are available on the ministry website at: www.slm.org.

Other books authored by Dr. Lambert and available from distributors and resellers worldwide currently include:

Charismatic Captivation—Authoritarian Abuse & Psychological Enslavement in Neo-Pentecostal Churches

Charismatic Control—Witchcraft in Neo-Pentecostal Churches

The Prophetic Gifts and Office—A Biblical Perspective

DUNAMIS! Power From On High!—Receiving the Baptism in the Holy Spirit

Mystery of the Kingdom—Bearing Kingdom Fruit

Made in the USA
Columbia, SC
28 November 2022

72193136R00048